Wintergreen Manuals

2016–2018

Wintergreen Manuals

2016–2018

Wintergreen Studios Press

Township of South Frontenac, PO Box 75, Yarker, ON, Canada K0K 3N0

Copyright © 2015 by Rena Upitis. All rights reserved under the International and Pan-American Copyright Conventions. No part of this book may be reproduced in any form or by electronic or mechanical means, including information storage and retrieval systems, without permission in writing from the publisher, except by a reviewer, who may quote brief passages in a review. The views expressed in this work are those of the author and do not necessarily reflect those of the publisher.

Every effort has been made to contact the copyright holders, artists, photographers, and authors whose work appears in this text for permission to reprint material. We regret any oversights and we will be happy to rectify them in future editions.

Book and cover design by Rena Upitis

Composed in Calibri and Gill Sans, typefaces designed by Monotype Typography.

Library and Archives Canada Cataloguing in Publication

Upitis, Rena. 1958–

Wintergreen Manuals/Rena Upitis

ISBN-13: 978-0991872213

ISBN-10: 0991872215

1. Education—General.

    I.   Title. Wintergreen Manuals: 2016-2018
Legal Deposit—Library and Archives Canada

Contacts for Systems Maintenance & Emergencies

Neighbours & friends:	David Hahn, Forest Farms	613 273 5545
	Miguel Hahn	613 273 6280
	Louise Cooper & Adam Turcotte	613 273 9876
	Karen Smereka (Perth)	613 284 4656
	Rob & Heather (log house)	613 273 9169
Executive Director:	Rena Upitis	613 533 6212 (W)
		613 377 6687 (H)
Other Board Members:	Katharine Smithrim	613 766 4153
	Helen Turnbull	905 342 5340
	Serena Manson	613 546 8851
	Larry Scanlan	613 536 5743
Operations Manager:	Diane Black	613 544 8268
Propane Re-fill:	Superior Propane	1 877 873 7467
	Billing account: 1116707	
Laneway Plowing:	Justin Martin	613 530 0773
	Françoise	613 273 6702
		613 483 8278 (cell)
	Glen McNichols	613 374 2800

Solar: *Contact for problems with solar panels, batteries, generator back-up, solar hot water heater. Company is Quantum Renewable Energy.*

	Eric Collins	613 217 0690
	Rick Rooney	613 546 2326
Plumbing:	Jamie Arthur	613 264 0752
		js.arthur@sympatico.ca
	Mike Hogan	613 531 1155
		Plumbingbymike@hotmail.com
Telephone:	WTC (Kingston & Westport)	613 273 2121
	If phone is down: support@wtccommunications.ca	

Wireless internet:	Xplornet	1 866 841 6001
Electrical:	Sean Craig	613 561 1426
Propane Boiler:	Eric Collins	613 217 0690
Generator:	Eric Collins, Quantum	613 217 0690
	Scott Truman, True Electric	613 353 7358
Appliance Repair:	Rowe Refrigeration & Appliances	613 548 4733
Woodstove:	Andrew Tietzen	613 539 9076
KFLA Health:	Joanne McGurn	613 279 2151 (W)
		613 634 1908 (H)
EXOVA:	Private water testing	613 634 9307

* * * * *

Wintergreen phone: **613 273 8745**

To access voice mail while in the lodge:

- Pick up receiver
- If there is an interrupted dial tone, there are messages
- Dial #98 for messages and follow voice mail instructions

To access voice mail remotely:

- Dial 613 507 0880
- After the prompt, enter our phone number: 613 273 8745 #
- After the prompt, enter our PIN: 78547 #

OPERATIONS MANUALS

Building Facilities

Gardens and Grounds

Mechanical Systems

HANDBOOKS

Human Resources, Programs, and Finance

Volunteer Kit

Emergency

Board of Directors

Table of Contents

Introduction to Building Facilities 2

The Wintergreen Lodge: Housekeeping 3
- Before guests arrive 4
- While guests are at the lodge 5
- Tear-down after an event 6
- Periodic cleaning and maintenance 7
- Spring and fall cleaning 8

The Wintergreen Lodge: Kitchen 9
- Before guests arrive 10
- Ongoing 11
- Breakfast 12
- Lunch 13
- Dinner 14
- Tear-down after an event 15

Outbuildings 16
- Parthenon 17
- Hobbit House 22
- Meadow Hut 28
- Beach House 29
- Outhouses 30
- Tenting Kitchen 30
- Smokehouse and Bake Oven 30
- Sauna 31
- Generator Shed & Cabin Storage Shed 31

Introduction to Gardens and Grounds 34

Gardens 35
- Perennial Flower Beds 36
- Vegetable Gardens 38
- Special Vegetable Gardens at Wintergreen 39

Grounds 46
- Road Maintenance 47
- Trails 48
- Paddy's Lake 49

Introduction to Mechanical Systems 52

Power 53
- Watering the batteries 54
- Manually starting and stopping the generator 57
- Equalizing the batteries 61
- Keeping an eye on the system and warning signals 66
- Maintaining a regular maintenance schedule 67

Heat 68
Convincing the boiler to start 69
Maintaining the woodstove 73

Water 74
How to shut off the water 75
How to turn on the water 78
Outdoor water 80
Water samples 82

Introduction to Human Resources, Programs, and Finance 85

Human Resources 86
Overview 86
Organization Chart 87
Board Committees 88
Job Descriptions: Permanent Part-Time and Casual Employees 89
Job Descriptions: Casual Contracts 104

Registration and Event Planning 108
Overview 108
Workshops 109
Dinner-Entertainment Events and One Day Gatherings 110
Weddings and Other Group Retreats 111
Private Cabin Retreats 112

Book Publishing: Wintergreen Studios Press 113

Marketing 116

Finance 117
Bookkeeping and Records 117
Donations 119

Appendices 120
Privacy Statement 120
Online Forms for Registration 121
Sample Contract for Workshop Instructor 131
Sample Letter to Workshop Participants 132
Sample Invoice 133
Sample Receipt for Charitable Donations 134
Chart of Accounts 135
Sample Comparative Income Statement 141
Sample Aged Accounts Receivable 143
Sample Monthly Budget Report to the Board of Directors 144

Volunteers at Wintergreen 149
What is in this Volunteer Kit? 150
What kinds of volunteer opportunities can I expect? 150
What kind of time commitment is expected from volunteers? 154
Volunteer placement procedures 154

- Volunteer rights and responsibilities 156
- How are volunteers recognized? 157
- OK—I'd like to volunteer. What do I do next? 158
- How to find us 158
- Why volunteer? 160
- Privacy Statement 161
- Wintergreen Studios Volunteer Application Form 162

Emergency Handbook 167
- Contact Numbers 167
- Additional Contacts for Emergencies 168

Fire Protocol 169
- Fire in Lodge 169
- Fire in Outbuildings 169
- Pre-Planning 169
- On Hearing the Alarm 169

Injury Protocol 170
- Pre-Planning 170
- In Case of Serious Injury 170

Incident Reports 171

General Overview of the Board of Directors 176

Board of Directors 178
- Organization Chart 181
- Board Committees 182

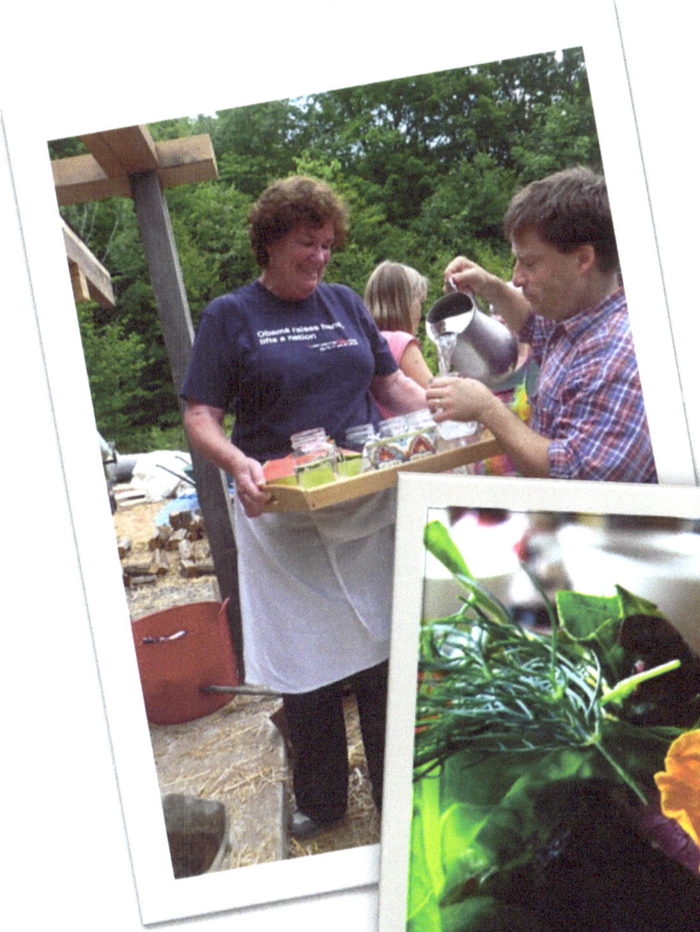

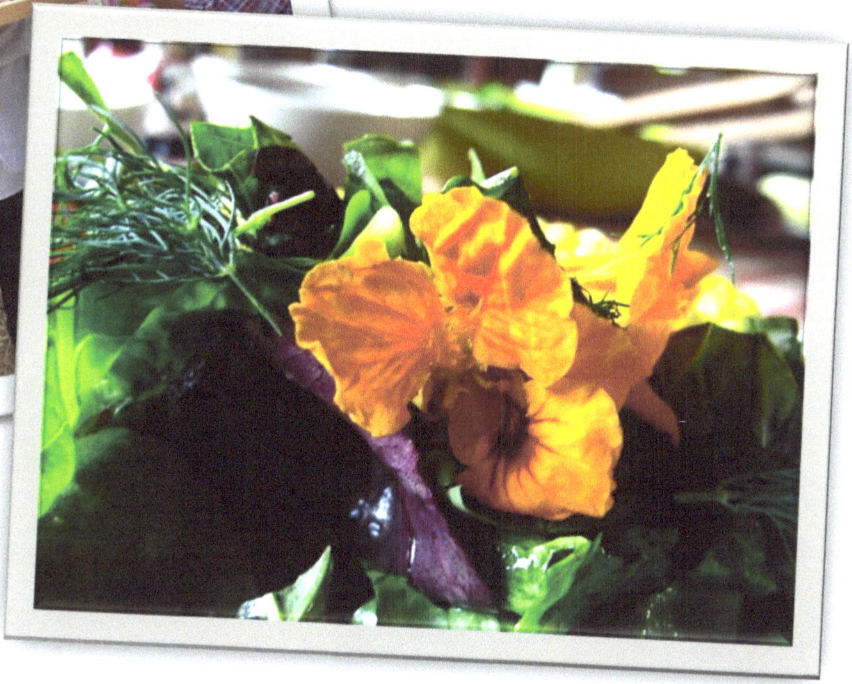

Operations Manual

Building Facilities

2016–2018

If you can't go where people are happier, try to make people happier where you are.

– Ashleigh Brilliant

Ideas without action are useless.

– Harvey Mackay

I long to accomplish a great and noble task, but it is my chief duty to accomplish small tasks as if they were great and noble.

– Helen Keller

Introduction to Building Facilities

This manual contains procedures and protocols for the interior operations of the Wintergreen lodge and outbuildings. Separate manuals detail operations for gardens and grounds, as well as maintenance of the off-grid mechanical, heat, and water systems.

The Operations Manager oversees the housekeeping and kitchen for the lodge and outbuildings. The Operations Manager also supervises contract kitchen and housekeeping staff that are hired, from time to time, to assist with workshops, retreats, and other events. The Operations Manager, in collaboration with the Executive Director and Education and Outreach Coordinator, also supervises kitchen and housekeeping volunteers.

The first section of this manual describes the **housekeeping** operations for the lodge, which include the cleaning and maintenance of bedrooms, bathrooms, common areas, and office/laundry area. The second section details the **kitchen** operations, which include the planning, preparation, and serving of meals as well as general kitchen cleaning and maintenance.

The third section describes the housekeeping and maintenance requirements for the outbuildings, which include guest cabins as well as cooking facilities, such as the smoke house and bake oven.

Extra copies of the most commonly used checklists are made available by the Operations Manager as needed.

The Wintergreen Lodge: Housekeeping

This section of the manual contains four checklists designed to assist with housekeeping tasks in the lodge, which are overseen by the Operations and Facilities Manager. They are as follows:

Before guests arrive
The bedrooms, bathrooms, and common areas must be clean and inviting when guests arrive for workshops, retreats, or other events. Normally, these areas are prepared after each event except for last minute details, such as flowers in the bedrooms and on the tables in the great rooms. Therefore, the preparation that takes place that is described in the first checklist assumes that the beds are already made, towels are in the bedrooms, floors are clean, and so on.

While guests are at the lodge
During an event, there are ongoing maintenance tasks that are listed on the second checklist. Most of these have to do with freshening the bathrooms and ensuring that the facilities remain clean and attractive during the event.

Tear-down after an event
The third checklist refers to the tear-down housekeeping tasks that occur at the end of a workshop or event, sometimes beginning before the session ends. For example, it is wise to try and start the laundry while guests are still in the lodge so that fresh sheets are available for making beds as soon as the guests depart.

Spring and fall cleaning
The final checklist details maintenance and cleaning tasks that take place in the spring and fall of each year when a thorough cleaning of the lodge occurs.

Before guests arrive

- ☐ check bedrooms and bathrooms for garbage, flies, dust

- ☐ wipe down bedroom and bathroom window sills

- ☐ flowers in bedrooms and bathrooms (in season)

- ☐ towels on beds (bath, hand, facecloth) in contrasting colours and two chocolates on towels

- ☐ check that beds appear neat (top sheets folded over, pillows over top sheets, duvets smoothed; matching pillow slips on double beds)

- ☐ check light switches (turning the switch by the door to the "on" position should turn on the table or floor lights in each of the bedrooms)

- ☐ check bathrooms for clean towels (beige, folded over once lengthwise), shower streaks, toilet cleanliness, general appearance

- ☐ shift furniture with instructor(s) as required; provide materials, such as data projector and screen, as needed

- ☐ salt & pepper, candles, and flowers on tables with cloths if workshop begins with dinner. If meal is later, have table settings ready (e.g., candles in holders)

While guests are at the lodge

- [ ] check bedrooms for garbage

- [ ] freshen bathrooms at 10 am; **replace towels,** clean toilets, showers, mirrors if required

- [ ] morning laundry (kitchen and bathroom towels)

- [ ] spot cleaning of floor in great room and kitchen

- [ ] photos and/or videos of participants (with permission)

- [ ] photos of food and food prep

- [ ] compost to green cones, outdoor compost, or garden as required (no meat in garden compost)

- [ ] recycling

- [ ] check battery voltage once or twice daily; see binder with parameter settings in mechanical room

- [ ] freshen bathrooms at 3 pm; **replace towels**, clean toilets, mirrors if required

- [ ] wood chopping (winter only)

- [ ] feed woodstove (winter only)

- [ ] weeding and gardening (spring, summer, fall only)

Tear-down after an event

- ☐ strip beds as early as possible (before guests leave)
- ☐ start laundry: sheets first
- ☐ begin making beds as soon as possible, with extra sheets on shelves in the staff bedroom.[1]
- ☐ put on raucous cleaning music after guests leave!
- ☐ tables: remove candles, salt & pepper
- ☐ top up salt & pepper and put in new candles if there is time to do so
- ☐ shake and/or wash table cloths
- ☐ bathrooms: empty garbage, clean toilets, sinks, mirrors, showers
- ☐ clean mirrors in great room, bathrooms, bedrooms
- ☐ clean glass (both sides) of main door and courtyard door
- ☐ bedrooms: remove flowers, dust, sweep as required when beds are made
- ☐ sweep and/or vacuum and/or steam wash bedroom, bathroom, and common area floors as required
- ☐ towels and napkins to launder (last)
- ☐ winter only: turn down heat (ranging between 55 and 62 degrees Farenheit) and shut off well and water – see Mechanical Systems Operations Manual
- ☐ new email contacts to Operations Manager or Executive Director

---

[1] Beds can be made with any of the sheets that fit—all of the colours are complementary, so there is no need to "match" bottom sheets with top sheets and pillowslips. The only exception is that for the double and king beds, the pillowslips should match one another. After fitting the bottom sheet, the top sheet is placed on the bottom sheet, smoothed as much as possible (the sheets will always be wrinkled because they are organic cotton), and then folded back. The pillow goes on top of the top sheet. The duvet should be placed as smoothly and evenly as possible on the bed, ensuring that the sheets do not show under the duvet cover. Each bed should have an ornamental pillow or two, which guests can also use as a backrest for reading.

Periodic cleaning and maintenance

These are tasks that need to be attended to more frequently than the spring/fall cleaning, but need not be done with each event or workshop. The Operations and/or Facilities Manager determines when these tasks should be completed.

- ❏ Sand and oil kitchen counters as required
- ❏ Check fire extinguishers monthly
- ❏ Check for spider webs monthly
- ❏ Window sills and other surfaces monthly
- ❏ Fill salt in water softener as required

Spring and fall cleaning

- [ ] spider webs
- [ ] windows (in and out)
- [ ] loft floor
- [ ] woodstove maintenance
- [ ] stove pipe and chimney cleaning schedule: Fall 2013, Fall 2015, Fall 2017, Fall 2019
- [ ] remove dishes, etc., and clean all kitchen cupboards
- [ ] full cleaning of bedrooms
- [ ] full cleaning of bathrooms
- [ ] sort cupboards
- [ ] wash floors and finish with polish
- [ ] beat rugs
- [ ] air and/or wash duvet covers
- [ ] air duvets
- [ ] wood cutting/stacking (NB – don't stack wood directly against lodge walls)

The Wintergreen Lodge: Kitchen

There are six checklists designed to assist with kitchen tasks in the lodge. They are as follows:

Before guests arrive
The kitchen should look organized (and busy in a lovely sort of way!), with snacks, washed fruit, coffee, tea, and water available when guests arrive.

Ongoing
During an event, there are ongoing maintenance tasks that are listed on the second checklist. Most of these have to do with preparation for upcoming meals and general kitchen maintenance. Note also the parallel "ongoing" checklist for housekeeping in the earlier section of the manual.

Breakfast
The third checklist details the items that need to be prepared for breakfast, including details about presentation of the meal.

Lunch
The fourth checklist details lunch planning and presentation.

Dinner
The fifth checklist details dinner planning and presentation as well as the tasks that need to be completed in the evening when breakfast is to be served on the following morning.

Tear-down after an event
The final checklist details tear-down tasks specifically related to the kitchen after an event is over. Note also the tear-down list for housekeeping in the previous section of the manual.

Before guests arrive

- ☐ ensure that the kitchen is as clean as possible
- ☐ snacks available in designated area
- ☐ aprons and caps are on
- ☐ fruit available and washed
- ☐ food put away and labeled according to upcoming meals
- ☐ allergies posted on fridge
- ☐ meals and recipes posted on fridge
- ☐ replenish list ready to go on fridge
- ☐ cookies or muffins or veggies and dip on arrival
- ☐ coffee (decaf and caf) in thermoses on arrival
- ☐ hot water in thermos on arrival
- ☐ cream and milk out (on ice) and labeled
- ☐ sugar with clean spoons and a vessel for dirty spoons
- ☐ prepare napkins and rings

Ongoing

- ❑ ensure that the kitchen is as clean as possible
- ❑ snacks are available in designated area
- ❑ check water level on jug; replenish lemon/lime slices daily
- ❑ spot cleaning of floor in great room and kitchen
- ❑ photos of food and food prep
- ❑ begin preparation of future meals
- ❑ keep an eye on ingredients that might need to be replenished/substituted
- ❑ weeding and gardening (spring, summer, fall only)
- ❑ leave kitchen clean in late evening
- ❑ EVENING: berries from freezer to fridge; bread to rise; load coffee

Breakfast

- ☐ make coffee & decaf coffee; transfer to thermoses

- ☐ hot water in thermos

- ☐ cream and milk next to thermoses

- ☐ water jug – new lemons/limes and *fresh water*

- ☐ juice and glasses

- ☐ yogurt (garnished with flowers if possible)

- ☐ granola in glass canister with dry measure scooper

- ☐ fruit (usually frozen berries; may supplement with fresh)

- ☐ jams, butter, and nut butters

- ☐ breads

- ☐ one main dish (e.g., baked eggs, French toast, scrambled tofu, pancakes)

- ☐ music – something classical (Bach) or folk (Sarah Harmer, David Francy …)

- ☐ set island with plates, napkins, cutlery & centerpiece

- ☐ set up three sinks (soapy, rinse, sanitize)

- ☐ announce breakfast

Lunch

- ❑ prepare dishes (three dishes + bread and dessert)

- ❑ water jug – new lemons/limes and *fresh water*

- ❑ set island with plates, napkins, cutlery & centerpiece

- ❑ label dishes according to dietary restrictions

- ❑ set up three sinks (soapy, rinse, sanitize)

- ❑ announce lunch

- ❑ dishes during meal if possible

Dinner

- ❏ prepare dishes (four to six dishes + bread and dessert)

- ❏ water jug – new lemons/limes and **fresh water**

- ❏ music – something jazzy – Miles Davis

- ❏ set island with plates, napkins, cutlery & centerpiece

- ❏ label dishes according to dietary restrictions

- ❏ set up three sinks (soapy, rinse, sanitize)

- ❏ announce dinner

- ❏ dishes during meal if possible

Tear-down after an event

- [ ] kitchen dishes – wash and store all items – *do not leave any dishes or pots drying in the racks*

- [ ] fridge – remove perishable leftovers, wipe down shelves and drawers

- [ ] stove – clean stovetop; oven only if required

- [ ] sinks – steel wool stainless sinks; bleach/polish/bleach porcelain sinks

- [ ] wash large coffee urn, if applicable, and ensure that the perculating mechanism is cleaned with the device that comes with the urn and/or vinegar

- [ ] wash coffee pots and thermoses; vinegar as required

- [ ] water jug – empty and dry completely; leave top off

- [ ] compost to be delivered to a green cone

- [ ] recycling to be removed off premises

- [ ] garbage to be removed off premises

- [ ] replenish list to Facilities Manager and/or Operations Manager and/or Executive Director, depending on the circumstances

- [ ] file recipes; remove allergy list

- [ ] sweep and/or vacuum and/or steam wash kitchen floors as required

- [ ] set mouse traps if required

Outbuildings

There is a separate checklist for each of the outbuildings. For the outbuildings that are most often used for personal retreats (Parthenon and Hobbit House), additional details regarding their access and use are provided. These documents, also available electronically, are provided to guests of the Parthenon and Hobbit House before arrival.

Parthenon
This section describes operations for guest stays as well as periodic maintenance. The document created for guests is also included. This document, titled "Directions, Tips, and Protocols for an Enjoyable and Safe Stay" is edited annually.

Hobbit House
This section describes operations for guest stays as well as periodic maintenance. The document created for guests is also included. This document, titled "Directions, Tips, and Protocols for an Enjoyable and Safe Stay" is edited annually.

Meadow Hut
This section describes operations for guest stays as well as periodic maintenance.

Beach House
This section describes operations for guest stays as well as periodic maintenance.

Outhouses
This section describes periodic maintenance.

Tenting Kitchen
This section describes periodic maintenance.

Smokehouse and Bake Oven
This section describes periodic maintenance.

Sauna
This section describes periodic maintenance.

Generator Shed and Cabin Storage Shed
This section describes periodic maintenance.

Parthenon

Before guests arrive

- ☐ laundered sheets placed in the flour bin or on the futon
- ☐ toilet paper
- ☐ kindling and wood available in the winter months
- ☐ dishes (pots, pans, cutlery, etc.) available and clean
- ☐ butane burner operational
- ☐ candles, kerosene lamps, and matches available

After guests leave

- ☐ remove sheets and launder; return to bin in staff room
- ☐ general check and clean for next guest (see above)

Periodic maintenance

- ☐ painting and carpentry as required
- ☐ check fire extinguishers spring and fall of each year
- ☐ stovepipe and chimney cleaning schedule:
    - ○ fall 2017
    - ○ fall 2019

PARTHENON

DIRECTIONS, TIPS AND PROTOCOLS FOR AN ENJOYABLE AND SAFE STAY

What to bring …

Our woodland cabins are a bit like elegant indoor camping. There is no running water, we use outhouses and thunder boxes, and cooking is primitive – but the beds are oh, so comfortable, and the buildings are warm and dry. The views of the forest, glades, and lake are spectacular.

There are no roads to our cabins. This means that you need to be prepared to hike from the main lodge (15 to 20 minutes) over some rough ground. Pack as if you were camping – except you can leave your dishes, tent, and linens at home! You should pack:

1. Sturdy walking shoes with ankle support and good treads.
2. A flashlight for each person (with extra batteries).
3. Bug spray and sunscreen.
4. First aid kit.
5. Personal toiletries, towel, and warm and waterproof clothes.
6. Drinking water and/or a filter if you plan to use lake water.
7. Food and ice-packs for cooling.
8. Cell phone if possible – our reception is limited, but there are open places where you can pick up a signal should you need to make an emergency call.
9. Matches.
10. Camera, journal, etc.
11. We recommend a backpack so that your hands are free during the walk.
12. Extra socks. Always pack extra socks! ☺

Risks and responsibilities …

While we do not anticipate you coming to any harm (in over 20 years, no one has been seriously hurt on this land), injury is always possible, especially in cold weather when the paths can be icy, or in the swimming and boating areas where appropriate cautionary measures should be taken. There are some rough areas to traverse. And there is an abundance of wildlife – beautiful birds, deer, beavers – and yes – occasionally a bear will pass through. We have been privileged to see a bear only twice in over two decades, and both times the bears were so frightened of us that we only caught a glimpse of them. These black bears are wild – completely undomesticated – and we want to keep them that way. Accordingly, do not leave any food at the cabin when you depart.

By choosing to stay at one of our woodland cabins, you agree to observe rules and instructions as outlined in this document and on our website. You also recognize that there are inherent risks associated with the wilderness and assume full responsibility for personal injury to yourself and companions (if applicable), and release and discharge *Wintergreen Studios* for injury, loss or damage arising out of your stay, whether caused by yourself, your companions, or other third parties. You further agree to pay for all damages caused by negligent, reckless or willful actions.

Please note that our cabins and property are STRICTLY NON-SMOKING.

Checking in ...

Generally no one will be staying in the cabin before or after you so check in times can be what works for your schedule or, if you need to meet with one of the staff before starting your stay, the check in time will have to be coordinated with the staff person as well. Check out time is as needed for your own schedule as well. There are no keys. If you have been to Wintergreen before, or if you're confident that you can make your way with these directions, often no one will meet you and you'll park your car and set out into the woods. But let us know if you want a staff person to meet you, and we'll arrange that with pleasure.

Hiking in ...

Once you have parked at the lodge, follow the rough gravel road behind the lodge, down the hill, to the opening on the south-west side of the meadow. You'll see the Meadow Hut on your right (pictured below). Keep walking for a few more meters until you reach the trailhead. This is the Main Trail, marked with red markers. The markers will be on your left as you hike towards the cabins and the lake (Left Lake, Right Returning).

There will be several trails coming off the Main Trail (South Trail, North Trail) before you reach the branch that will take you past the Hobbit House, on the way to the Parthenon (see Hobbit House marker, pictured). The Parthenon is about 4 minutes past the Hobbit House (turn left at the bottom of the hill at the back side of the Hobbit House, and join the Stream Trail – yellow markers). It's about 20 minutes to the Parthenon in total when the trail isn't covered with ice or snow. The Parthenon is close to the lake – you can see it through one of the big Parthenon windows.

On the following two pages [*not included in the Operations Manual*], you'll find maps of the property. Not only will these help you find the Parthenon, but they'll also give you an idea of the hikes that you can enjoy during your stay.

The Parthenon! (and Matilda, who will be there to greet you...)

Once you've arrived …

There is a double futon on the main floor of the Parthenon, and a single mattress in the loft. The ladder to the loft is right behind the "kitchen," hanging on the wall. There are two slots in the floor to secure the ladder in place. Bedding is in the round cylindrical barrel – we keep it in there to keep the mice out. You might want to bring a couple of extra sleeping bags if it's really cold. Alternately, you'll find more bedding in the main cabin – help yourself.

There's an outhouse not far from the Parthenon, to your right as you face out the front door.

You can cook on the woodstove or on the one-plate burner. The burner uses butane fuel, which freezes at -10 Celsius. Please follow the directions that come with the burner. If you can't get the burner to work, you'll have to resort to the woodstove (not such a terrible way to cook!).

Speaking of the woodstove… it's an easy one to light, but because it is not airtight, it also gets extremely hot, so be mindful of that. It also goes out quickly, but the Parthenon is well insulated, so once you get it warm, it will stay warm for some time.

To start the woodstove, simply put lots of crumpled newspaper in through the top, followed by kindling and two smallish pieces of wood. Then light from BELOW – there's a little trap door at the very bottom of the stove. It will whoosh into life. The trap door, below, can be used to regulate the air flow – lots at first, with the door slid fully open. Then add wood from above as needed.

You may enjoy a campfire in the campfire ring at the cabin next door if there isn't a fire ban in place. Please inform yourself about the fire conditions of South Frontenac County before your stay (see http://www.township.southfrontenac.on.ca). It's usually easy to collect deadfall for the fire from the woods.

When you leave, please be sure to close the door securely to keep woodland creatures from using the cabins!

Emergency protocol …

If something happens to someone in your party, do not move him/her. Keep the person warm and comfortable. Make contact with 911 or Louise Cooper (613 273 9876) or David Hahn (613 273 5545), our nearest neighbours, either at the site or back at the lodge. If the lodge is unoccupied, you should be able to pick up a cell phone signal in the parking lot.

Hobbit House

Before guests arrive

- ☐ laundered sheets placed in the cupboard
- ☐ toilet paper
- ☐ kindling and wood available in the winter months
- ☐ dishes (pots, pans, cutlery, etc.) available and clean
- ☐ butane burner operational
- ☐ candles, kerosene lamps, and matches available

After guests leave

- ☐ remove sheets and launder
- ☐ general check and clean for next guest (see above)

Periodic maintenance

- ☐ painting and carpentry as required
- ☐ check fire extinguishers spring and fall of each year
- ☐ stovepipe and chimney cleaning schedule:
    - o fall 2017
    - o fall 2019

HOBBIT HOUSE

DIRECTIONS, TIPS, AND PROTOCOLS FOR AN ENJOYABLE AND SAFE STAY

What to bring ...

Our woodland cabins are a bit like elegant indoor camping. There is no running water, we use outhouses and thunder boxes, and cooking is primitive – but the beds are oh, so comfortable, and the buildings are warm and dry. The views of the forest, glades, and lake are spectacular.

There are no roads to our cabins. This means that you need to be prepared to hike from the main lodge (15 to 20 minutes) over some rough ground. Pack as if you were camping – except you can leave your dishes, tent, and linens at home! You should pack:

1. Sturdy walking shoes with ankle support and good treads.
2. A flashlight for each person (with extra batteries).
3. Bug spray and sunscreen.
4. First aid kit.
5. Personal toiletries, towel, and warm and waterproof clothes.
6. Drinking water and/or a filter if you plan to use lake water.
7. Food and ice-packs for cooling.
8. Cell phone if possible – our reception is limited, but there are open places where you can pick up a signal should you need to make an emergency call.
9. Matches.
10. Camera, journal, etc.
11. We recommend a backpack so that your hands are free during the walk.
12. Extra socks. Always pack extra socks! ☺

Risks and responsibilities ...

While we do not anticipate you coming to any harm (in over 20 years, no one has been seriously hurt on this land), injury is always possible, especially in cold weather when the paths can be icy, or in the swimming and boating areas where appropriate cautionary measures should be taken. There are some rough areas to traverse. And there is an abundance of wildlife – beautiful birds, deer, beavers – and yes – occasionally a bear will pass through. We have been privileged to see a bear only twice in over two decades, and both times the bears were so frightened of us that we only caught a glimpse of them. These black bears are wild – completely undomesticated – and we want to keep them that way. Accordingly, do not leave any food at the cabin when you depart.

By choosing to stay at one of our woodland cabins, you agree to observe rules and instructions as outlined in this document and on our website. You also recognize that there are inherent risks associated with the wilderness and assume full responsibility for personal injury to yourself and companions (if applicable), and release and discharge *Wintergreen Studios* for injury, loss or damage arising out of your stay, whether caused by yourself, your companions, or other third parties. You further agree to pay for all damages caused by negligent, reckless or willful actions.

Please note that our cabins and property are STRICTLY NON-SMOKING.

Checking in …

Generally no one will be staying in the cabin before or after you so check in times can be what works for your schedule or, if you need to meet with one of the staff before starting your stay, the check in time will have to be coordinated with the staff person as well. Check out time is as needed for your own schedule as well. There are no keys. If you have been to Wintergreen before, or if you're confident that you can make your way with these directions, often no one will meet you and you'll park your car and set out into the woods. But let us know if you want a staff person to meet you, and we'll arrange that with pleasure.

Hiking in …

Once you have parked your car, follow the rough gravel road behind the lodge, down the hill, to the opening on the south-west side of the meadow. You'll see the Meadow Hut on your right (pictured below). Keep walking for a few more meters until you reach the trailhead. This is the Main Trail, marked with red markers. The markers will be on your left as you hike towards the cabins and the lake (Left Lake, Right Returning).

There will be several trails coming off the Main Trail (South Trail, North Trail) before you reach the branch that will take you to the Hobbit House. It's about a 15-minute hike to the Hobbit House Trail, which is marked in orange-ish-pink markers, again on the right.

On the following two pages [*not included in Operations Manual*], you'll find maps of the property. Not only will these help you find the Hobbit House, but they'll also give you an idea of the hikes that you can enjoy during your stay.

Once you've arrived …

When you reach the glade where the Hobbit House is located, you'll see a fire pit (which you are welcome to use) as well as the thunder box in the distance, just beyond a pine tree. Firewood is under the roofing panels in the glade.

The only tricky thing inside the Hobbit House is making up the bed. When you arrive, it will be a window seat. The linens are in the cupboard on the left (pictured – but they may be a different colour – we have great flannel sheets in red, purple, yellow, etc.). The legs for the bed are in the same little cupboard.

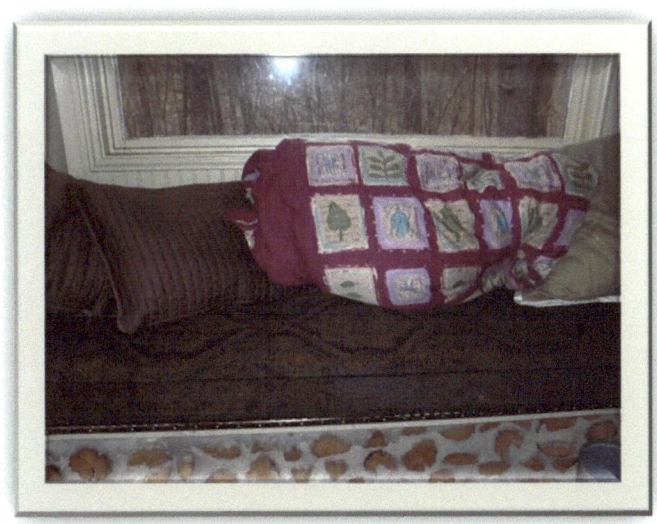

To assemble the bed, remove the cushions and put the legs in the rectangular slots (they're numbered 1 through 3, and work best in that order!).

Pull down the bed from there, and assemble cushions and linens (the brown zippered sleeves are hiding proper pillows!). If you have the woodstove going, be mindful that the bed is quite close to the stove. The stove will go out in the night at any rate, and the Hobbit House will be very warm if you run the stove for a few hours.

Speaking of the woodstove… you can cook on the stove, outdoors, or on the one-plate burner. There is extra fuel up on the top shelf in a blue canister.

You may enjoy a campfire in the fire pit if there isn't a fire ban. Please inform yourself about the fire conditions of South Frontenac County before your stay (see http://www.township.southfrontenac.on.ca).

Enjoy!! It's a magical place… the lake is down the hill behind the Hobbit House, up the Stream Trail (mustard yellow).

When you leave, be sure to secure the door. Our biggest challenge is keeping the mice out of our lovely buildings!

Emergency protocol …

If something happens to someone in your party, do not move him/her. Keep the person warm and comfortable. Make contact with 911 or Louise Cooper (613 273 9876) or David Hahn (613 273 5545), our nearest neighbours, either at the cabin site or back at the lodge. If the lodge is unoccupied, you should be able to pick up a cell phone signal in the parking lot.

Meadow Hut

Before guest arrives

- ☐ single bed made with sheets and coverings
- ☐ kindling and wood available in the winter months
- ☐ candles, kerosene lamps, and matches available

After guest leaves

- ☐ remove sheets and launder
- ☐ general check and clean for next guest (see above)

Periodic maintenance

- ☐ painting and carpentry as required
- ☐ check fire extinguishers spring and fall of each year
- ☐ stovepipe and chimney cleaning schedule:
    - o fall 2017
    - o fall 2019

Beach House

Before guests arrive

- ☐ make up futon or provide laundered sheets
- ☐ kindling and wood available in the winter months
- ☐ candles, kerosene lamps, and matches available
- ☐ general cleanliness – sweep, etc.

After guests leave

- ☐ remove sheets and launder
- ☐ general check and clean for next guests (see above)

Periodic maintenance

- ☐ painting and carpentry as required
- ☐ check fire extinguishers spring and fall of each year
- ☐ stovepipe and chimney cleaning schedule:
    - fall 2017
    - fall 2019

Outhouses

There are two outhouses on the property, one near the Paddy's Lake Cabin (which is also used by guests of the Parthenon), and another in the tenting area. There is also a thunder box near the Hobbit House. No outdoor facilities are near the Meadow Hut or the Beach House. Guests of these facilities use the Main Lodge.

Outhouses need to be checked for cleanliness once a month, and toilet paper should be provided in the tenting meadow outhouse. The outhouse near Paddy's Lake Cabin only has toilet paper on the holder when there are guests present. Otherwise, toilet paper is stored in the nearby cabins.

Both outhouses should have a supply of hand sanitizer at all times.

Tenting Kitchen

The tenting kitchen, when in use, should have propane and a burner, bleach for dishes, and the rain barrel hooked up for dishwater. Shelves should be wiped clean before guests arrive.

Smokehouse and Bake Oven

The smokehouse and bake oven require little maintenance. Before operating the smokehouse, check that the stovepipe is securely connected and that the only items in the smokehouse are the drying racks and the items to be smoked. The towels for cleaning the bake oven are stored in the laundry area of the lodge. Care should be taken in emptying the bake oven of hot ashes.

Sauna

The sauna should be swept out before use. A supply of kindling and small pieces of wood should be kept under the bench, along with paper for starting the fire. Matches are kept in the ante- chamber. To start the fire, open the ash bin to encourage a strong draw. This can be used to regulate the heat, along with the damper on the stovepipe. The window can also be opened to cool the sauna as required.

Provide water for the sauna in a non metallic jug (it gets hot!). Towels can be taken from the lodge.

Please remind guests that they should limit their time in the sauna to 15 or 20 minutes, and that no alcohol should be consumed in the sauna.

The sauna should not be used by pregnant women or people with high blood pressure.

Generator Shed & Cabin Storage Shed

Storage sheds require yearly organizing and cleaning. Check the generator shed, periodically, to ensure that there is oil for the propane generator, a funnel, and gas for the lawn mower and gas generator. There should also be a gas/oil mixture for the trimmer and chainsaw.

The gas generator should be stored in the shed whenever possible, along with the cable that connects the gas generator to the main lodge. The gas generator is a back-up to the propane

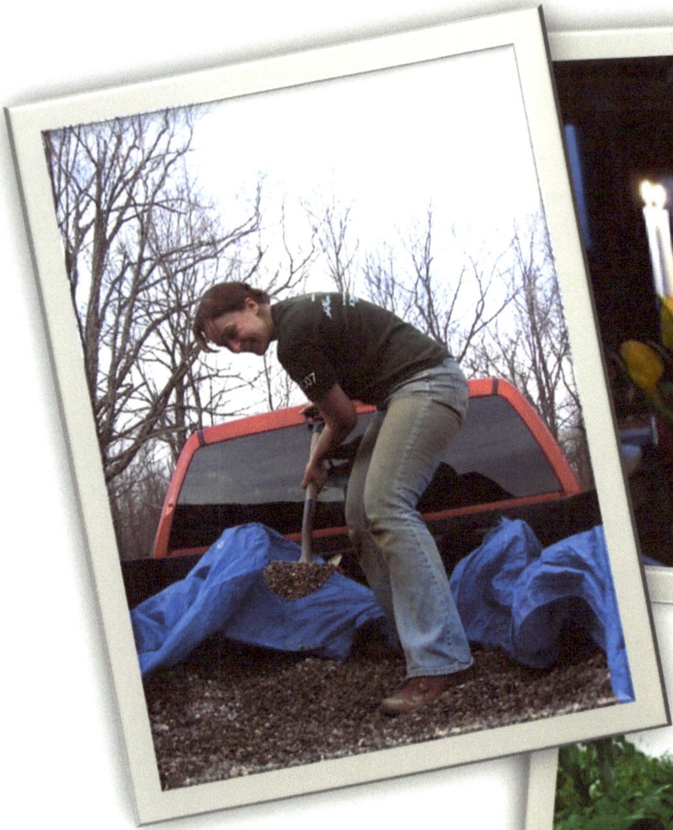

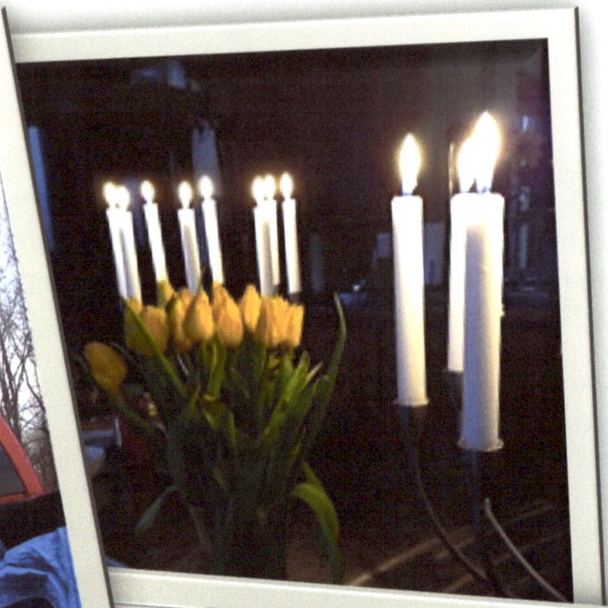

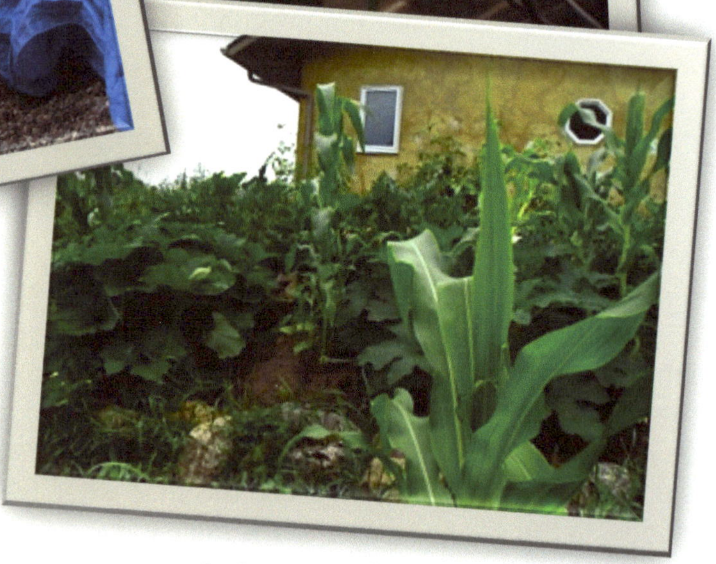

Operations Manual

Gardens and Grounds

2016–2018

If you can't go where people are happier, try to make people happier where you are.

– *Ashleigh Brilliant*

Ideas without action are useless.

– *Harvey Mackay*

I long to accomplish a great and noble task, but it is my chief duty to accomplish small tasks as if they were great and noble.

– *Helen Keller*

Introduction to Gardens and Grounds

This manual contains procedures and protocols for the gardens and grounds around the lodge and the small outbuildings throughout the Wintergreen land, as well as the system of trails that run through the 204 acres of property.

The Facilities Manager and Operations Manager collaborate to ensure that the gardens and grounds are maintained. The Facilities Manager also supervises contract gardens and grounds staff who are hired, from time to time, to assist with the maintenance of the gardens and grounds. The Facilities Manager, in collaboration with the Education and Outreach Coordinator, supervises all volunteers.

Gardens

There are two checklists designed to assist with gardening. They are as follows:

Perennial Flower Beds
There are spring, summer, and fall duties associated with the perennial flower beds. In the winter, they sleep!

Vegetable Gardens
The vegetable gardens require intense work in the spring and steady maintenance in the summer. The checklist gives a framework of what can be expected.

Special Vegetable Gardens at Wintergreen
We sometimes, on a year-by-year basis, create gardens that are used for school tours and workshops. Information used for workshops about two of our gardens, the Three Sisters Garden and the Victory Garden, is provided in this section. We have also experimented with straw bale gardens and a Spaghetti Garden, featuring tomatoes, herbs, and onions.

Perennial Flower Beds

Spring

- ☐ Hook up the rain barrel.

- ☐ Weed, weed, weed! (but be careful, as some of the tender perennials may be hiding under the mulch

- ☐ Maintain paths and add new pea gravel as required

- ☐ Split and transplant perennials as needed to thin plants and fill in bare spots

- ☐ Even though we have mostly perennial gardens, there are a few annuals to plant:
    - Nasturtiums
    - Cosmos
    - Sunflowers
    - … and possibly Love-in-the-mist & hyssop & …

- ☐ Flowers in the big pots are also generally annuals. In the pot on the west side, early spring plantings might include pansies and greens from the forest. Later in the spring, begonias and ivy do well.

- ☐ The front planters get a lot of sun, so plant annuals accordingly. Peach coloured geraniums and variegated green and white plants are a possibility.

- ☐ Mow and trim as required, as often as once a week in the early spring. Make sure the mowing is done to coincide with events.

- ☐ Mulch as required. There can never be too much mulch!

- ☐ Bare patches in the garden can receive vegetable-based compost from the kitchen (the rest goes in the green cones or in the garden compost bins on the way to the Beach house).

- ☐ Remove poison parsnips **WITH GLOVES**.

- ☐ Trim bushes and lilacs as required.

Summer

- ☐ Weeding is less intense, but still important to do regularly.

- ☐ Water as required (the more mulch, the less watering).

- ☐ Watch for poison parsnips – pull from the roots **WITH GLOVES**.

Fall

- ☐ Cut back plants as required.

- ☐ Disconnect rain barrel.

- ☐ Ensure all tools are properly stored for the winter months.

Winter

- ☐ Read books about perennials, order seeds, dream of spring!

Vegetable Gardens

Spring

- ☐ Prepare gardens as required with mulch, manure, straw, soil

- ☐ Start seedlings indoors

- ☐ Begin early plantings (e.g., radishes) in late April or early May

- ☐ Plant according to recommendations for each type of vegetable, ensuring that gardens are rotated from year to year.

- ☐ Our most successful plants include:
    - Tomatoes
    - Squash (including zucchini)
    - Onions
    - Lettuce greens
    - Bush beans
    - Scarlet runner beans

- ☐ A variety of herbs, both perennial and annual, should also be grown each year.
    - Dill
    - Coriander
    - Rosemary
    - Lemon Balm
    - Lovage
    - Thyme
    - Sage
    - Lamb's ears (mostly ornamental)
    - Chives
    - Parsley

Special Vegetable Gardens at Wintergreen

There are several featured gardens at Wintergreen that form part of the school tours and curriculum support materials. These are grown most years, and are as follows:

- Three Sisters
- Victory Garden
- Spaghetti Garden

Additional information about these gardens appears on the following pages.

What is a Three Sisters garden?

Six Nations peoples (Haudenosaunee, pronounced hah-dee-no-show-nee, and meaning "People of the longhouse") have used a wide range of agricultural techniques. Perhaps the best known is a garden planted with corn, beans, and squash together—a trio of companion plants referred to as the "three sisters." Wintergreen has a Three Sisters Garden on the west side of the lodge.

In a Three Sisters garden, **beans, corn,** and **squash** help each other grow.

1. Beans have tiny **bacteria** living on their roots that help absorb **nitrogen** from the air and soil. Nitrogen helps corn grow strong and tall.
2. Corn provides **support** for beans by acting like a beanpole.
3. The large, prickly squash leaves **shade the soil**, preventing weed growth, and deter animal pests.

These gardens—considered special gifts from the creator—played an important role in the **agriculture** and **nutrition** of many Six Nations peoples and other farming nations throughout North America. Considered a **survival garden**, families could survive the long winter from the fruits of the Three Sisters!

How do I plant a Three Sisters garden?

Plan and select a site. You'll want to plant your Three Sisters garden in late spring once the danger of frost has passed. Choose a site that has **direct sunshine** for most of the day and access to water.

Prepare the soil. First, break up and rake the soil. Next, build a **mound** about **30 cm high** and **1 meter in diameter**. Mounds should be **1 to 1.5 meters apart** in all directions.

Plant corn. Soak four to seven corn seeds overnight and then plant them about **15 cm apart** in the center of each mound. Many Six Nations people honor the **tradition** of giving thanks to the "Four Directions" by orienting the corn seeds to the north, south, east, and west.

Plant beans and squash. After a week or two, when the corn is at least **10 cm high**, soak and then plant six pole bean seeds in a circle about **15 cm** away from the corn. At about the same time, plant four squash or pumpkin seeds next to the mound, about a foot away from the beans.

Maintain your traditional garden. As corn plants grow, weed gently around them and mound soil around the base of each stem for support. When the corn is knee-high and again when **silks** appear on the husks, **side-dress** by putting a **high nitrogen fertilizer** (such as aged manure or fish emulsion) on the soil surface near each plant. If beans aren't winding their way around the corn, you can help by moving **tendrils** to the stalks. If you pinch off the tips of squash runners after several fruits have started to form, the plants will devote more **energy** to producing squash.

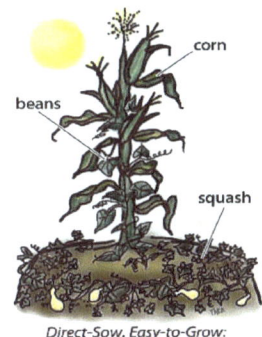

Direct-Sow, Easy-to-Grow:
The Ancient **Three Sisters** Method

What seeds are the best to plant?

Here are some different varieties you can try. Many seed packets have a picture of the vegetable on the front, to help you decide.

Corn	Beans	Squash
TEXAS HONEY JUNE	SCARLET RUNNER	ZUCCHINI
BLACK IROQUOISE	TRUE CRANBERRY	ACORN SQUASH
BLACK AZTEC	HOPI PURPLE SNAP BEAN	LONG PIE PUMPKIN

How do I save the seeds for next season?

By **saving** and **replanting** some of the seeds from their Three Sisters gardens, Six Nations cultures brought the **cycle of life** full circle. You can save the seeds for next year, or give some to other gardeners. Make sure you store the seeds in an airtight container somewhere cool and dry! Here's how to do it:

Corn	Beans	Squash
Leave several ears on the stalk until husks dry and turn brown. Remove and peel back the husks and hang them to dry, out of direct sun, for a month. Once they're dry, remove the individual kernels.	Leave several pods on a plant until they turn brown and brittle. Break open the pods and remove the seeds. Leave them on a flat surface or screen, out of direct sun, to air dry for a few days.	Scoop out the seeds with a spoon and rinse them with water in a colander. Follow the same instructions as listed for drying and storing beans.

Three Sisters Soup

5 cups water	2 cups corn kernels
2 cups green beans, chopped in 1-inch length	2 cups diced, peeled butternut squash
1-1/2 cups diced, peeled potatoes	2 cups diced boneless pork (optional)
2 tbsp butter, at room temperature	2 tbsp all-purpose flour
3/4 tsp salt	1/2 tsp pepper

In large pot, **combine** water, corn, beans, squash, potatoes and pork (if using). **Bring to boil** over high heat. **Reduce heat** to medium-low; cover. **Simmer** 10 minutes or until vegetables are almost **tender**. In small bowl, **mash** together flour and butter. **Stir** into soup. Increase heat to medium. **Cook**, stirring, 5 minutes or until vegetables are tender. Stir in salt and pepper. Makes about **6 servings**. (From the *Toronto Star*, Nov 30, 2005, C03.)

References and Resources

- Anon. (2001). A three sisters garden. *Green Teacher, 65*, 18.
- Erney, D. (1996). Corns, beans, and squash…long live the three sisters. *Organic Gardening, 43*(37), 5–11.
- National Gardening Association (2002). *Growing ideas: Classroom projects*. Retrieved from http://www.kidsgardening.com/growingideas/projects/march02
- Three sisters (agriculture). *Wikipedia*. Retrieved from http://en.wikipedia.org/wiki/Three_Sisters_%28agriculture%29
- Vivian, J. (2001). The Three Sisters. *Mother Earth News, 184,* 50–55.

This project was supported by Queen's University and the Government of Canada/FedDev Ontario, the Frontenac Community Futures Development Corporation (FCFDC), and the Social Sciences and Humanities Research Council of Canada (SSHRC), and in partnership with Earthworx, Compostec, and the Worm Factory.

Victory (Wartime) Gardens

During World War II, the United States had to ship large amounts of food overseas to feed the troops. At the same time, many farmers had joined the military and could not look after their farms. This meant there was not as much food available for people to eat. The government created a Victory Garden campaign to promote home gardening. Growing a Victory Garden was a way for people at home to grow nutritious food and feel patriotic, too. Wintergreen's Victory Garden is modeled after a mid-sized garden typically found in Pennsylvania during WWII.

People plowed backyards, vacant lots, parks, baseball fields, and schoolyards to set out their Victory gardens.

These gardens were planted with easy-to-grow vegetables, fruits, and herbs. The goal was to produce enough fresh vegetables through the summer for the immediate family and neighbors. Any excess produce was canned and preserved for the winter and early spring until next year's Victory garden produce was ripe.

- During World War I and II, Victory Gardens were planted in America, Canada, the United Kingdom, and Germany.
- There were nearly 20 million Victory Gardens in America alone and these gardens produced 40% of the nations's food supply.
- Children and adults fertilized, planted, weeded, and watered in order to harvest an abundance of vegetables.

What can I plant in a Victory Garden?

The keys to planting were to choose crops that took little space (so no potatoes or corn) and that were easy to grow. Here is a list of vegetables you might try:

Leaf Vegetables	Root vegetables	Stalk Vegetables and Legumes	Bulb Vegetables	Fruits
Leaf lettuce, Kale, Head Lettuce, Boston Lettuce, Cabbage, Swiss Chard, Mustard Greens	Carrots, Yellow Turnips, Radishes, Celeriac, Parsnip	String Beans, Dwarf Peas, Lima Beans, Edible Soy Beans	Onions, Spring onions, Leeks	Tomatoes, Cucumbers, Sweet Peppers

Who can tell me more about Victory gardens?

Many senior citizens will know about Victory Gardens. They might have even grown one. You can become a journalist and interview a senior citizen who had a Victory Garden to learn more about why they were important. You might interview a grandparent, a war veteran, or someone at a local senior citizens home. Remember to ask politely, and to write a thank you card when you are done. Plan your interview before hand, and practice with a friend first. Here are some questions you might ask:

- What is different between gardening now and when you were young?
- Where did you grow your Victory Garden?
- What was the best or worst thing you remember about your Victory Garden?

More things to do...
- Compile your interview segments into an oral history "program" to share with other classes, your elder friends, or to stream on your Web site, or create a book from these stories with your commentary.

- Design a garden using ideas, plants, or techniques described by your elder friends. Perhaps they can even help you work on it!

Cooking with Victory Garden Produce

There are literally thousands of recipes you can create from a Victory Garden. Marian Morash wrote a book full of such recipes.

Grated Sautéed Beets and Carrots

4 medium beets

2 medium carrots

4T. butter or olive oil

fresh lemon juice

salt & pepper to taste

chopped fresh dill or parsley

Wash, peel, and coarsely **grate** the beets. **Melt** butter in a frying pan, add beets and carrots to **coat** with butter, and **sprinkle** with lemon juice to taste. **Cover** and cook for 10 minutes, cooking until just **tender**. Season and **garnish** with remaining ingredients.

_____

References and Resources

- Victory Garden Seed Company (2010). *The Victory Garden.* Retrieved from http://www.victoryseeds.com/TheVictoryGarden
- For images of WWII posters and advertisements, see http://www.fruitfromwashington.com/History/harvest.htm
- National Gardening Association (2010). *Living history: Interviewing elder gardeners.* Retrieved from http://www.kidsgardening.com/Dig
- Victory Gardens Handbook of the Victory Garden Committee War Services, Pennsylvania State Council of Defense (1944). Retrieved from http://www.earthlypursuits.com/VictoryGardHandbook
- Victory Garden (2010). *Wikipedia.* Retrieved from http://en.wikipedia.org/wiki/Victory_garden
- Morash, M. (2010) *The Victory Garden Cookbook.* NY: Knopf.

This project was supported by Queen's University and the Government of Canada/FedDev Ontario, the Frontenac Community Futures Development Corporation (FCFDC), and the Social Sciences and Humanities Research Council of Canada (SSHRC), and in partnership with Earthworx, Compostec, and the Worm Factory.

Grounds

There are three checklists designed to assist with grounds maintenance. They are as follows:

Road maintenance
This section describes both the winter and summer road maintenance tasks.

Trails
This section describes the trail maintenance procedures and schedules.

Paddy's Lake
This section describes the trail maintenance procedures and schedules.

Road Maintenance

Overall, the road requires little maintenance.

Winter

- [ ] In the winter months, when plowing is needed, call either Justin Martin (613 530 0773) or Françoise (613 273 6702 or 613 483 8278). Check each winter to see who is most available, and at the best price.

Spring and Summer

- [ ] Ensure that foliage that has grown over the road is cut back. Technically, there should be 22 clear feet across to allow for emergency vehicles.

- [ ] Ensure that the Wintergreen Studios sign is visible from both the north and south approaches on Canoe Lake Road.

- [ ] Top up and grade with gravel as required.

Trails

The thirteen trails are on a rotating system for clearing and cutting back. Each trail is maintained once in the three-year cycle, with the exception of the Main Trail, which is trimmed every year. Below is the schedule for 2013–2015:

2016

- ❏ Main Trail (red)
- ❏ Mica Mine Trail (green)
- ❏ Rainbow Ridge (blue)
- ❏ Southeast Corner Trail (mustard)
- ❏ Pine Trail (blue)

2017

- ❏ Main Trail (red)
- ❏ Marsh Trail (red)
- ❏ North Trail (orange)
- ❏ Lee's Marsh (mustard)
- ❏ Hobbit Trail (pink)

2018

- ❏ Main Trail (red)
- ❏ South Trail (orange)
- ❏ Cliff Trail (yellow)
- ❏ Stream Trail (mustard)
- ❏ Land Bridge

To maintain the trails, do the following:

- ❏ Toss dead wood off trail
- ❏ Cut back new growth with clippers
- ❏ Remove large dead fall with chain saw
- ❏ Re-spray and/or re-paint markers with the colours indicated above

Paddy's Lake

The area near the Main Cabin is where most visitors access Paddy's Lake. It is important that the waterfront is clean, safe, and accessible.

Spring

- ☐ Put cedar floating dock back in the water (takes at least two people).
- ☐ Put extended dock back in the water (takes at least two people).
- ☐ Perform any necessary repairs on docks.
- ☐ Clean boats and perform any necessary repairs. At present, there are two boats; a turquoise canoe and a yellow rowboat, called the Spring Peeper, that can also become a sailboat. The sail is kept in the loft of the Paddy's Lake Cabin. The floating dock can also be paddled out into the water.
- ☐ Ensure that there are paddles for the canoe and oars for the row boat.
- ☐ Ensure that there are at least 6 "noodles" near the lake area.
- ☐ There are three children's life jackets and two adult life jackets available for use. These are stored in the shed near Paddy's Lake Cabin.
- ☐ Hook up rain barrel next to Paddy's Lake Cabin.

Fall

- ☐ Remove cedar floating dock from the water (takes at least two people) by dragging it up as far as possible on the shore.
- ☐ Remove extended dock from the water (takes at least two people) by dragging it up over the fixed dock on the shore.
- ☐ Ensure that paddles and oars have been returned to the shed.
- ☐ Ensure that noodles and life jackets have been returned to the shed.
- ☐ Disconnect rain barrel.

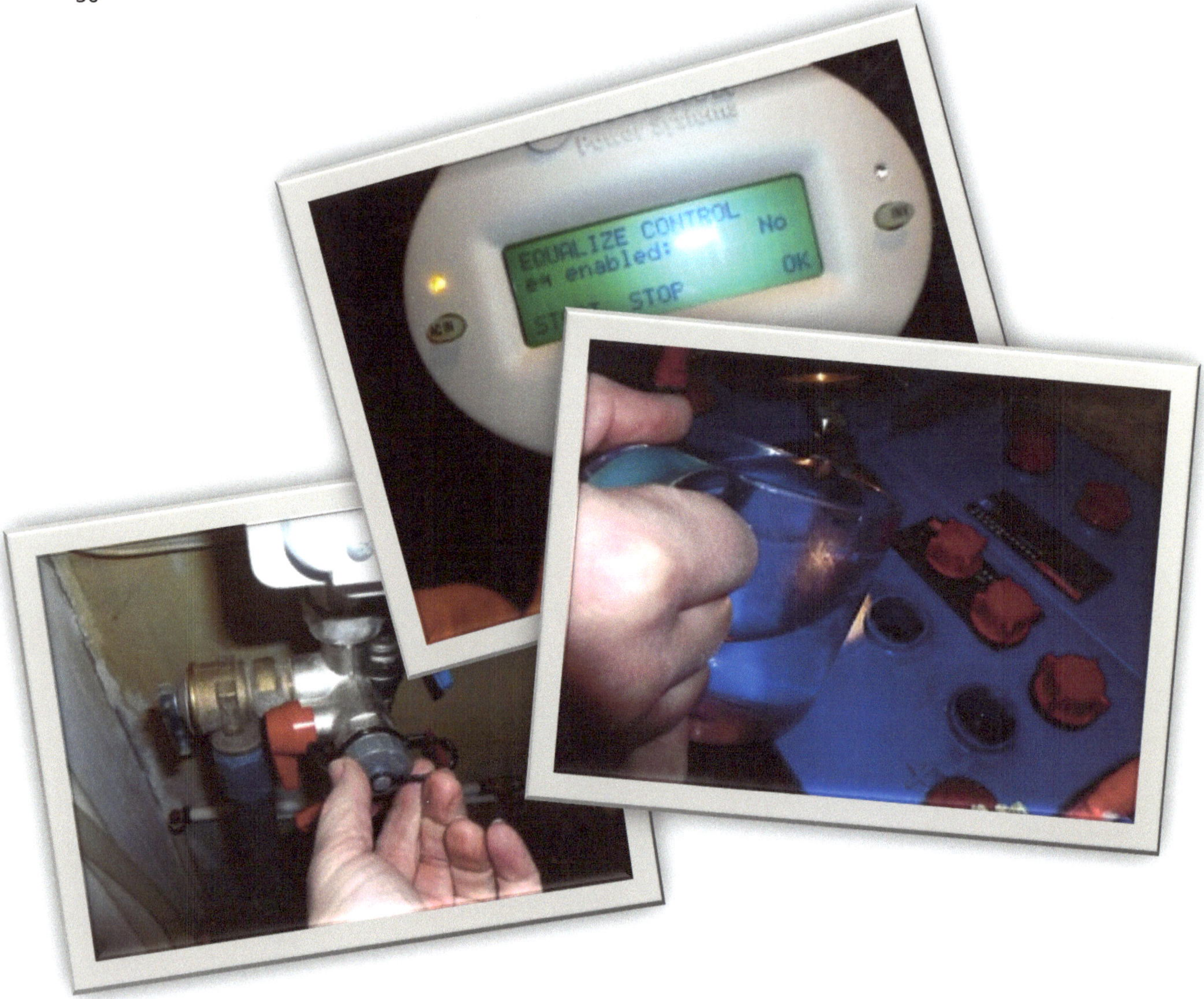

Operations Manual

Mechanical Systems

2016–2018

If you can't go where people are happier, try to make people happier where you are.

– *Ashleigh Brilliant*

Ideas without action are useless.

– *Harvey Mackay*

I long to accomplish a great and noble task, but it is my chief duty to accomplish small tasks as if they were great and noble.

– *Helen Keller*

Introduction to Mechanical Systems

This manual contains procedures and protocols for the mechanical systems pertaining to the Wintergreen lodge. These include the power system (batteries, back up generators, charge controller, etc.), the heating system, and the water systems.

The Facilities Manager oversees the maintenance and operations of the mechanical systems. The Facilities Manager, in collaboration with the Education and Outreach Coordinator, also supervises volunteers associated with the mechanical system, both in terms of its operation and in terms of educational outreach activities.

Power

This section contains five sections, as described below.

Watering the batteries
The batteries require regular watering to ensure that the level of water covers the plates contained in the batteries.

Manually starting and stopping the generator
Although the generator should start automatically if there isn't enough charge in the batteries from solar power, from time to time there is a need to start and stop the generator manually. For example, this procedure is followed when equalizing the batteries.

Equalizing the batteries
From time to time the batteries need to be equalized to help maintain the life of the batteries and the efficiency of the system. This section of the manual describes how to equalize the batteries.

Keeping an eye on the system and warning signals
From time to time, during the day when the lodge is in use, it is prudent to ensure that the power supply is reliable. This section of the manual descries these procedures.

Maintaining a regular maintenance schedule
Regular maintenance of the batteries (see above) as well as the back-up generator and tankless hot water system are required. This section provides a schedule of tasks and timelines for regular maintenance.

Watering the batteries

The batteries need to be watered approximately once a month, possibly more in the summer.

STEP 1: Remove both covers from the two shelves of batteries (eight on each shelf). The top cover lifts right off, as shown; the bottom cover folds down.

 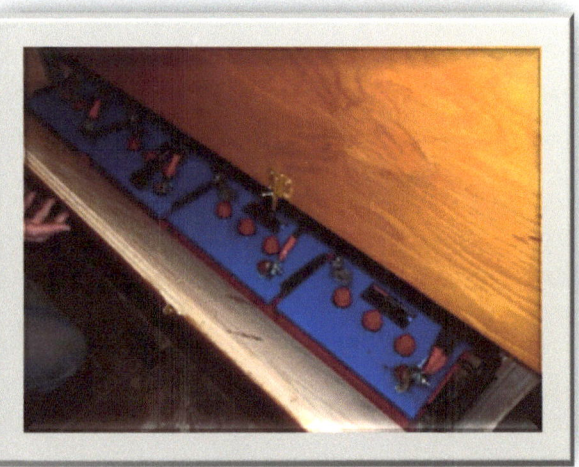

STEP 2: Remove the red caps to water the batteries. You might want to remove the caps in sections and then replace them 6 at a time to help remember which ones have been done, but any systematic approach is fine. Be careful not to drop any of them – they are a pain to get out (with salad tongs!).

STEP 3: Using distilled water and the plastic measuring cup, fill the batteries until the water is just starting to come up the neck of the cylinder as shown. Replace caps and plywood covers when you're done.

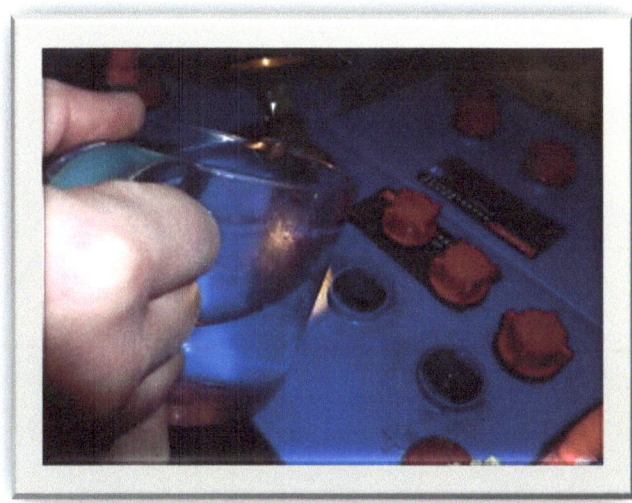

STEP 4: Clean up spills on the floor and around the batteries themselves. There are rags in the room on the shelves against the outside wall (remember, it's sulfuric acid and water in those batteries, so don't wear your best velvet garb to do this job).

STEP 5: Enter the date that the batteries were watered into the systems log, along with the amount of water that was needed. If there is less than 8 litres of distilled water remaining in storage, add distilled water to the replenish list on the kitchen fridge.

Manually starting and stopping the generator

The generator *should* come on automatically if the battery voltage drops too low according to the pre-set parameters. For example, the generator comes on if the voltage drops below 47.6 for two minutes (a coffee percolator and vacuum cleaner running at the same time on a cloudy day will set it off); 48.4 V for two hours, or 49.2 V for 24 hours. The generator will run, then, until the batteries reach 58.6 V and stay that way for two hours.

However, sometimes the generator has a mind of its own, and needs to be prompted. Also, one needs to start the generator manually when performing the equalizing function through the inverter (rather than through the charge controller).

The manual start is performed through the white oval control panel on the inverter. It will look something like one of the two photos below (numbers will vary, depending on the actual voltage and whether there is any draw on the system when you begin setting the generator).

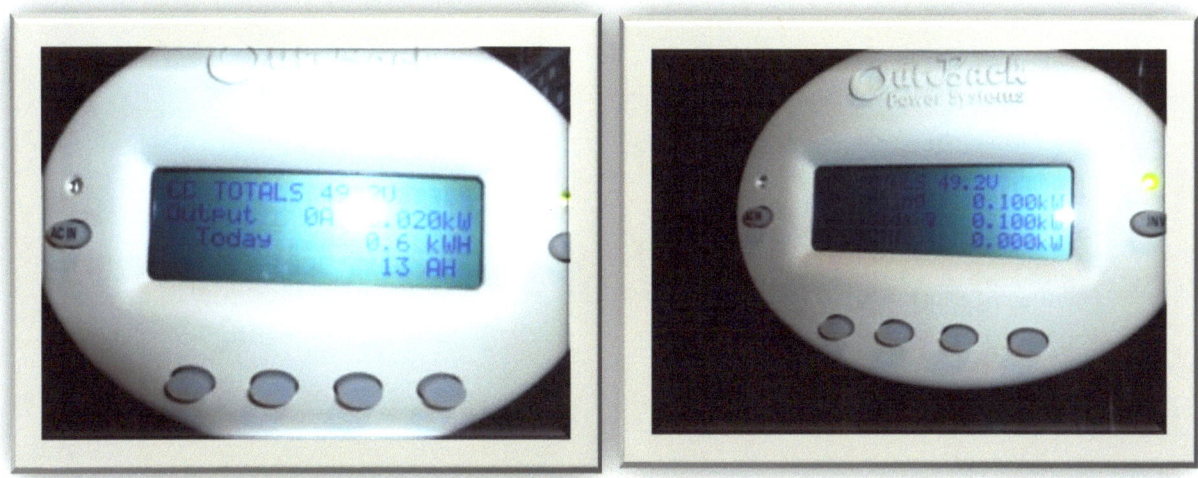

STEP 1: Press the button on the left side, as pictured. You'll need to press it *twice* until you reach the generator start panel (pictured on the right, below). The second line will read "currently: AUTO-OFF.

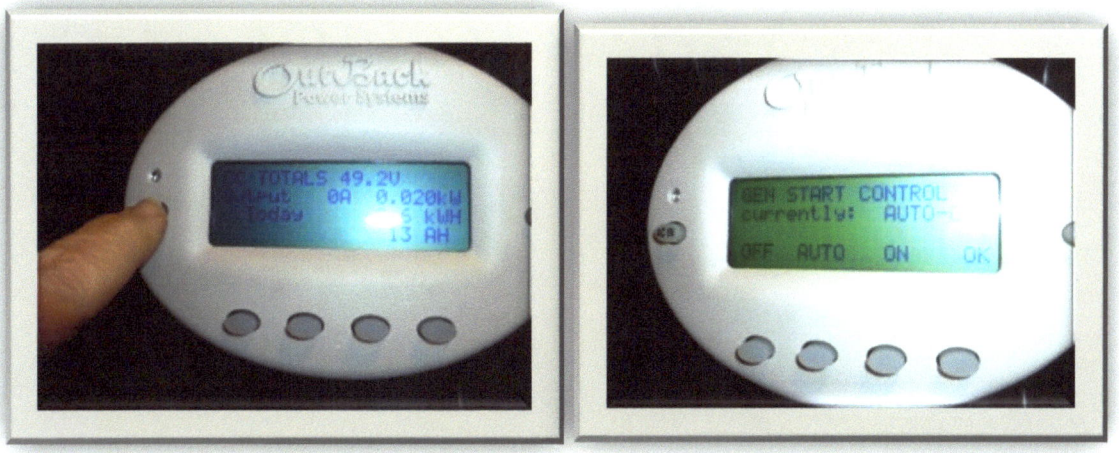

STEP 2: Press the ON button. When you do this lots of lights will flash on the panel to your left (see below), and in less than a minute, the light on the right will turn yellow, indicating that there is AC power coming in from the generator. Also, the panel display will change to "currently: MAN-ON."

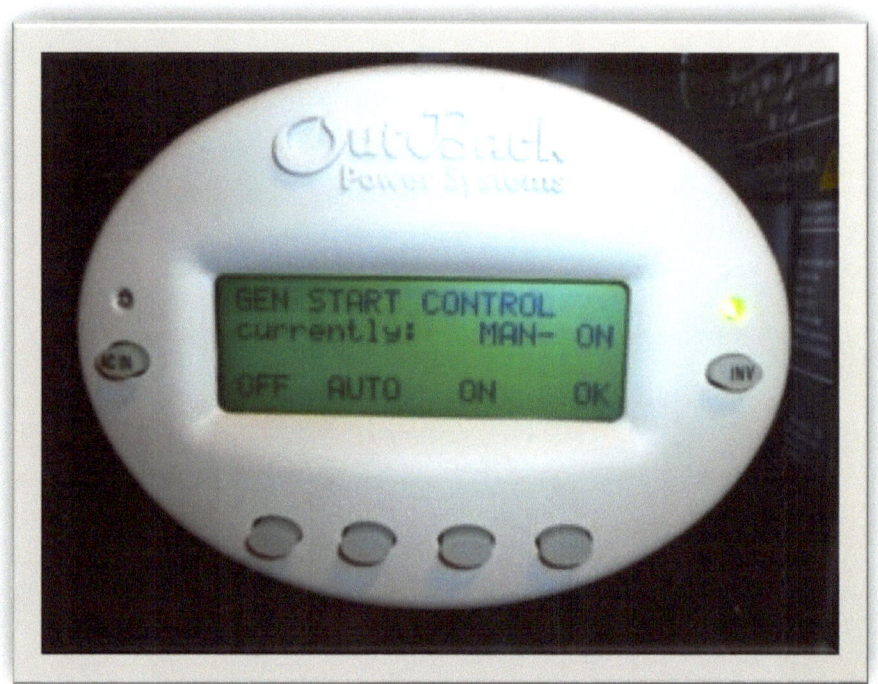

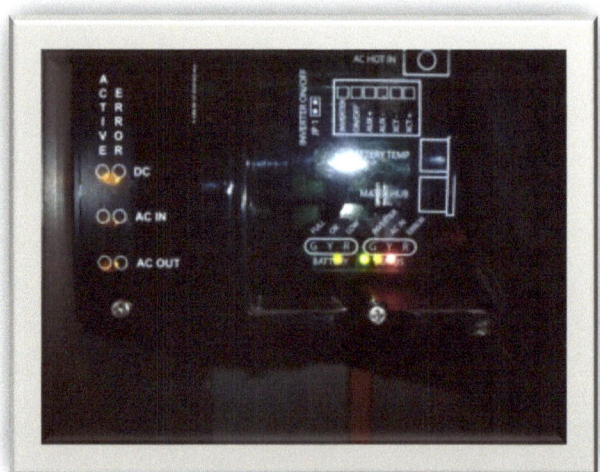

STEP 3: You'll have to decide how long to run the generator. If you have started the generator because the batteries were low, it is best to run it for a couple of hours AFTER it reaches 58.6 V. If it has trouble reaching 58.6 (say, it takes more than two hours), then just run it for a couple of hours at about 54 V. If you are running the generator to perform an equalizing charge, the voltage should reach 62.4 for an hour before the equalizing charge ends and the generator is manually shut off. However, the equalizer rarely gets that high – on a good day, it goes to 61.4. So after an hour at that voltage, it's time to turn off the generator.

STEP 4: To shut off the generator, return to the generator screen (see STEP ONE, above). Then press OFF as pictured on the left, below, resulting in the screen pictured on the right.

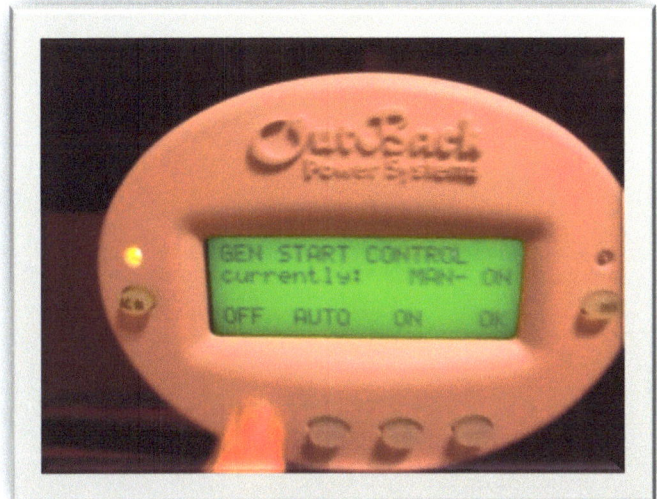

STEP 5: Press AUTO as pictured on the left, below, so that the generator comes on automatically the next time (yeah, right!). Then you will see the screen on the right.

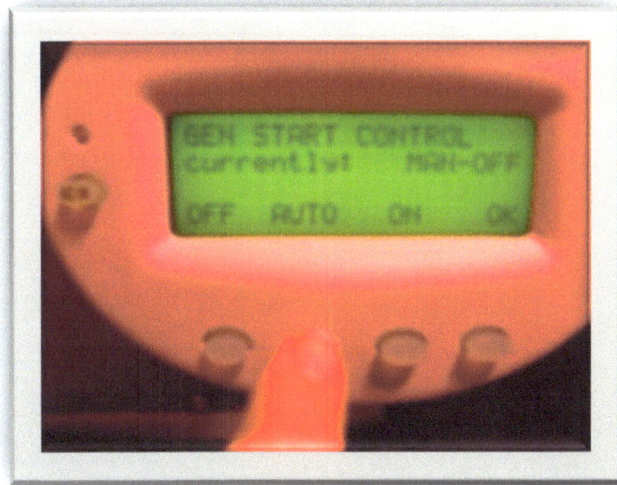
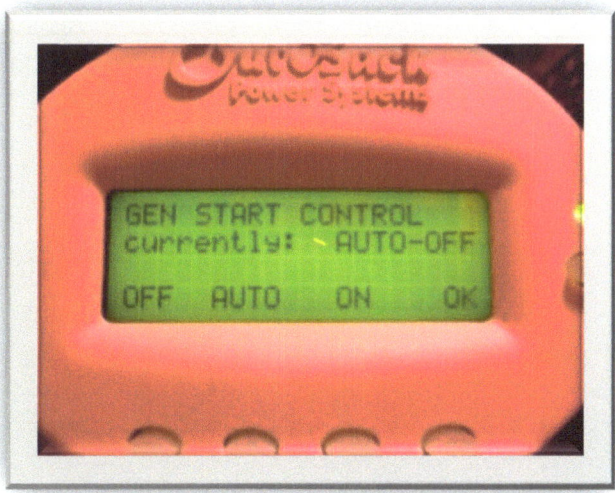

STEP 6: Return to the main menu by pressing the two left buttons simultaneously, and then pressing "SUM" as pictured below:

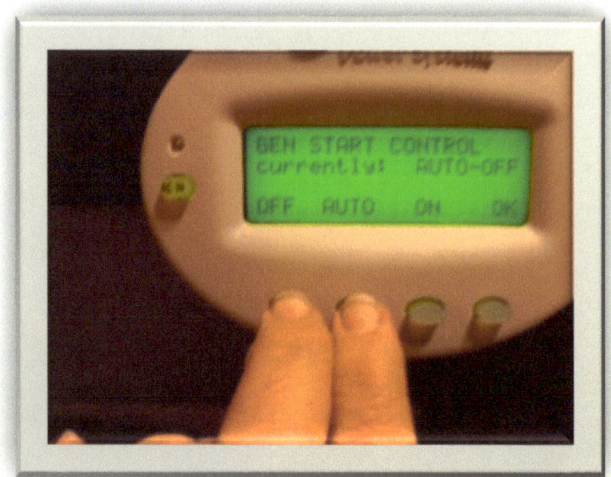

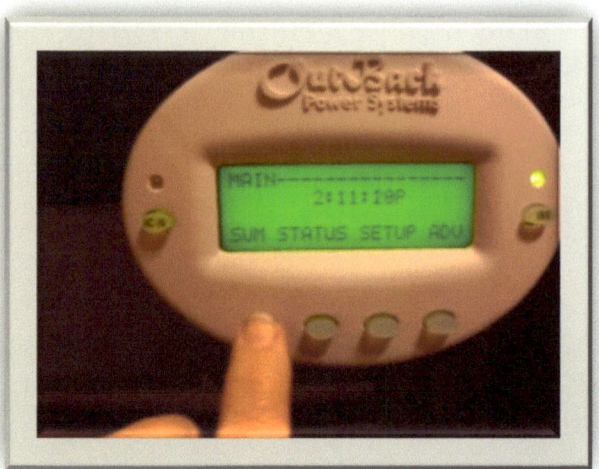

You're done! The summary screen will probably look something like this (with over 50V because the generator has been on):

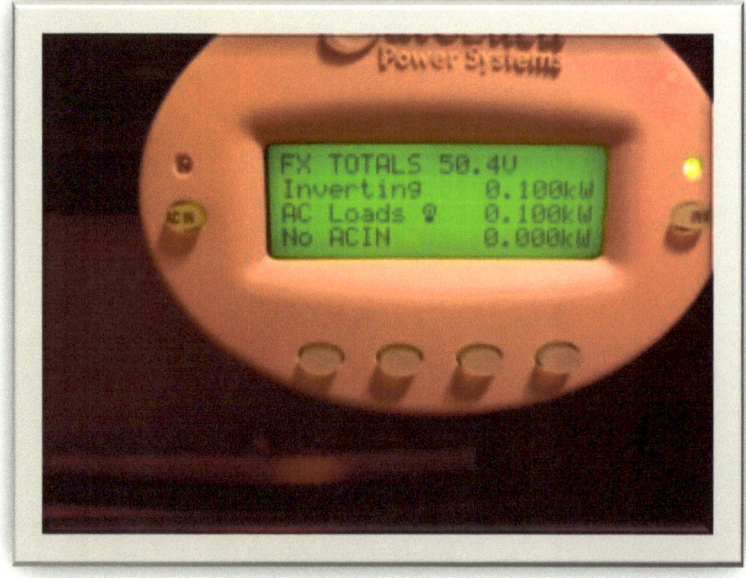

STEP 7: Enter the details in the logbook about the why you had to start and/or stop the generator, the voltage that was achieved, and the length of time that the generator was required.

Equalizing the batteries

The batteries need to be equalized at least once every few months (really, it means BOILING them!). Here's how you do it using the inverter, affectionately known as the "mate." Batteries can also be equalized through the charge controller directly.

STEP 1: Manually start the generator (see p. 8).

STEP 2: Press the button on the left side of the "mate" as pictured. You'll need to press it up to *four times* until you reach the equalizer start panel (pictured on the right, below), depending on where you start on the series of screens. Sometimes, you'll only need to press twice if you've just started the generator and the generator screen is still visible.

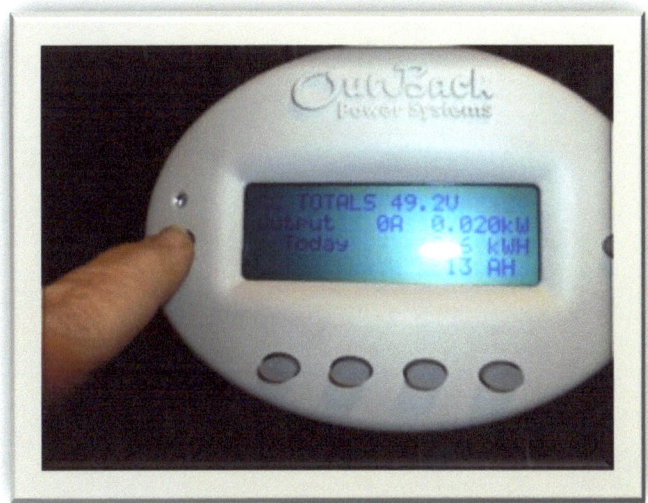
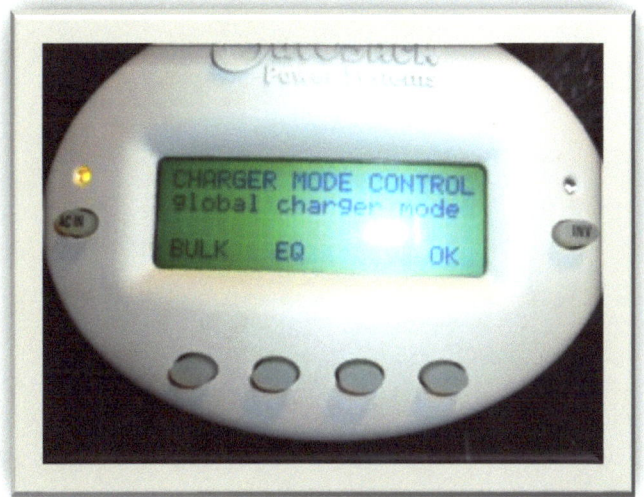

STEP 3: Press the EQ button.

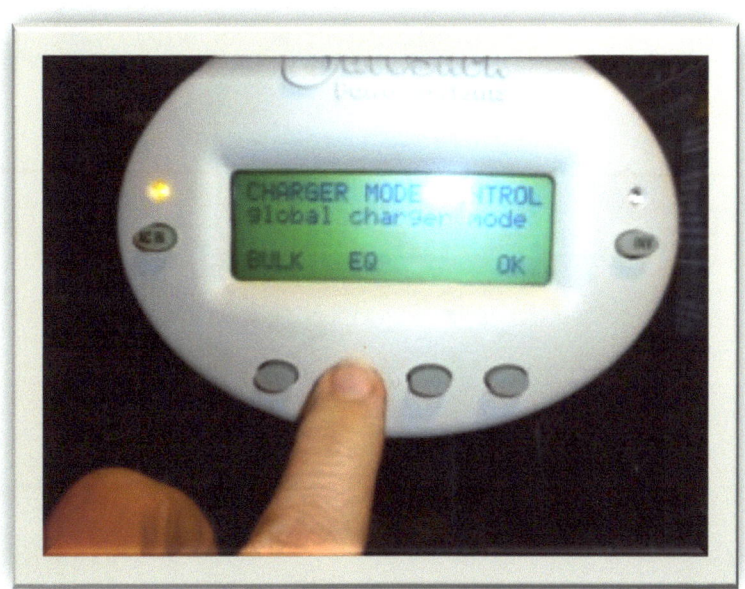

STEP 4: Press START *(or press STOP if you are ending the sequence; see Step 7, below)*.

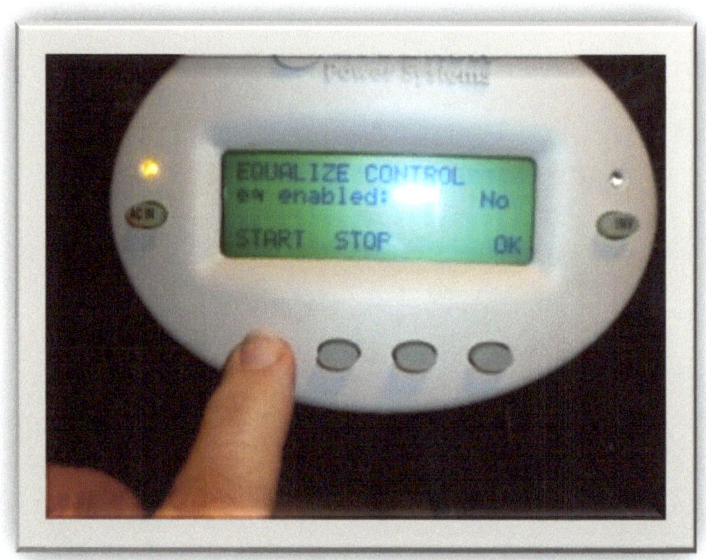

STEP 5: Press MORE twice.

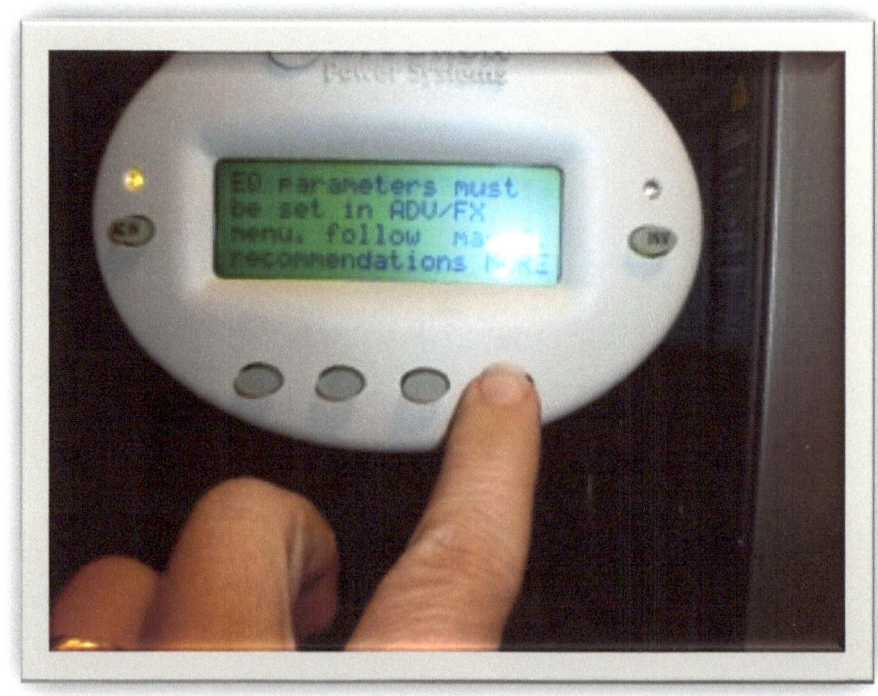

STEP 6: Press YES as pictured on the left, which will produce the screen on the right.

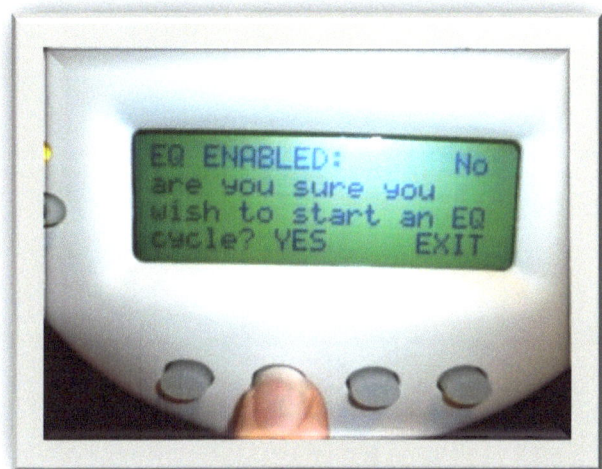 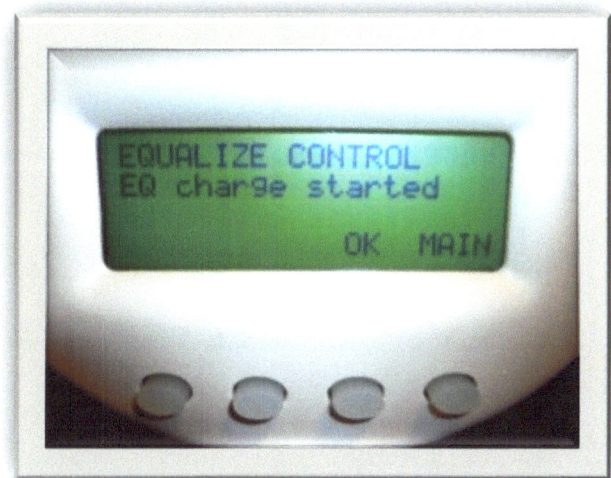

STEP 7: Go back to the main menu as pictured below, press SUM, and watch the voltage rise (bottom photo).

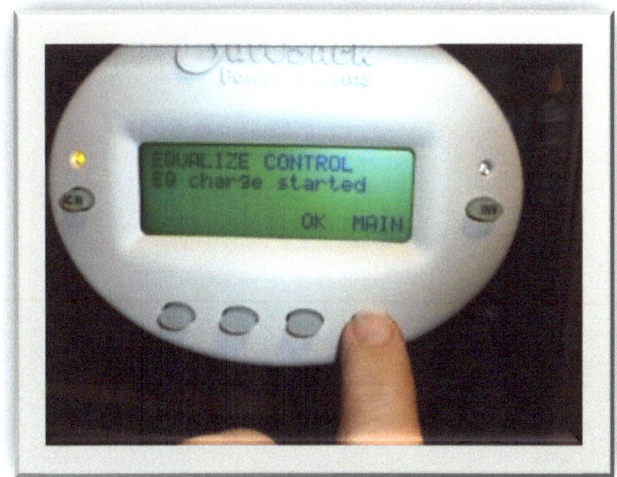 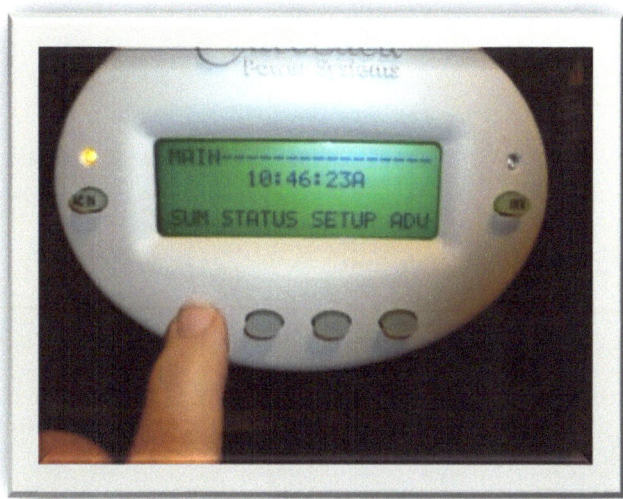

The voltage will rise as much as the generator and batteries will allow. In an ideal world, it will run for an hour at 62.4. Then the equalizer charge will shut itself off. But this is not an ideal world. If it has been stuck at anything over 60 for an hour, it *might* shut itself off, it might not. If it runs for five or six hours and it's not getting higher, stop the equalizing. To stop the equalizer, follow Steps 2, 3, 4, above, and then go to Step 8 to turn off the generator manually (which you have to do anyway).

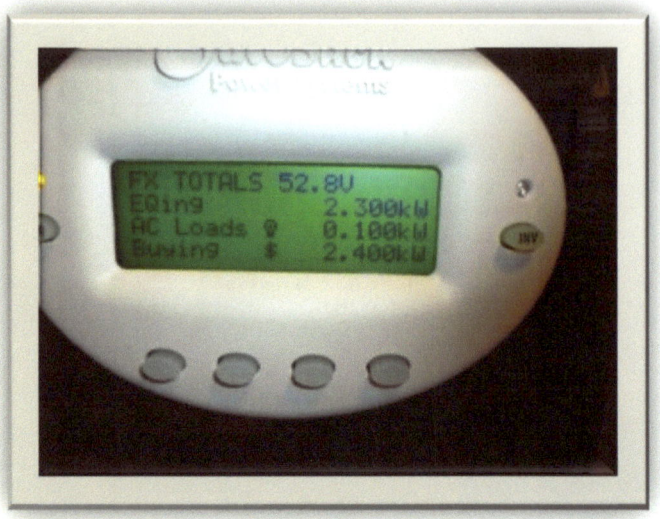

STEP 8: Turn off the generator manually (see separate instructions).

STEP 9: Return to the main screen by pressing the two buttons on the left simultaneously. Then press "SUM".

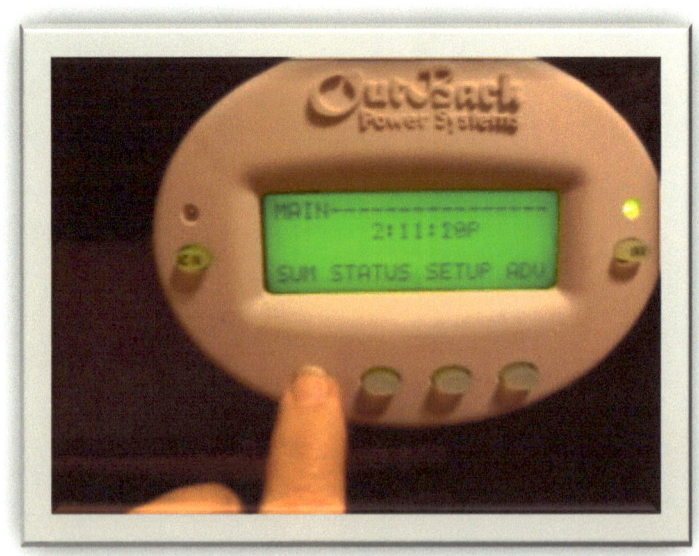

You're done! The summary screen will probably look something like this (with over 50V because the generator has been on).

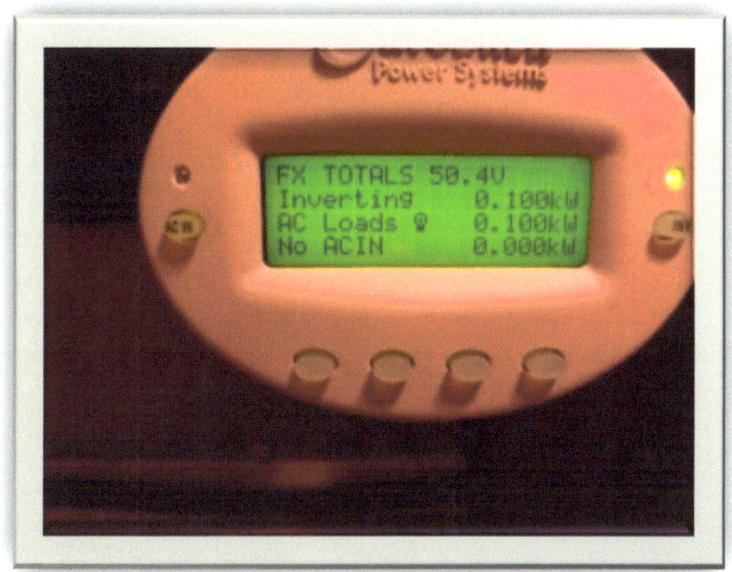

STEP 10: Enter the details in the logbook about the equalizing process in the log including the date, the voltage that was achieved, and the length of time that the generator was required.

Keeping an eye on the system and warning signals

From time to time, during the day when the lodge is in use, it is prudent to ensure that the power supply is reliable. Generally, the batteries should sit at around 50 V or higher. There are various set points that alert the generator to start, should the batteries fall too low (see set points in the manual in the mechanical room). If the voltage goes to 49.2 V for a 24 hour period, the generator should come on. Similarly, if the voltage drops to 48.4 V for two hours, or to 47.6 for two minutes, the auto function on the generator should kick in. This doesn't always work, which is why it is a good idea to pay attention to the battery voltage, especially if there is an event going on that draws a lot of power (including speakers, equipment, cooking, etc.).

There is an electronic warning system that sends email and voice mail messages to the service technician (Eric Collins) as well as to the Facilities Manager and Executive Director. These warnings include a drop in indoor temperature, a malfunctioning generator, and a malfunctioning boiler. Daily messages are also sent to the joint operations account (wintergreenstudios99@gmail.com).

Maintaining a regular maintenance schedule

Solar Panels
The solar panels on the roof of the lodge need little maintenance. However, in the winter months, if safe, it is a good idea to sweep the snow off the panels, accessing the roof from the courtyard. *The panels on the pole need to be kept clear all winter.* Also, the pole panels are tilted twice a year. In the winter they are in the steep position (second hole from the bottom), and in the summer, the flat position (second hole from the top). It takes four people to safely tilt the panels.

Propane Generator
Check that the oil is topped up every two months. Fill propane tank as needed (usually once a year at the most). Levels below 20% are critical. See the front of the manual for contact numbers for propane delivery.

Large Green Propane Tank for Lodge
Fill propane tank as needed (usually once in the late fall). Levels below 20% are critical.

Woodstove
Clean stovepipe in the fall of every odd year (i.e., 2017, 2019, etc.).

Boiler
Have it serviced every fall (see front of manual for contact numbers).

Heat

This section contains two documents, as described below.

How to convince the boiler to start
The boiler in the propane room controls the in-floor radiant heating. The propane room is next to the mechanical room where the batteries are housed. Sometimes, when the back-up generator has been on, the boiler doesn't start. This section explains how to re-start the boiler.

Maintaining the woodstove
This section of the manual describes how to use and maintain the woodstove.

Convincing the boiler to start

The radiant in-floor heating, controlled by the boiler in the propane room, will not work if the generator is running, and often will not start after the generator has been on. It simply interrupts the cycle, and there's no way to get it going again other than manually. Sometimes it's a simple matter of flicking the switch on the wall of the propane room marked "boiler" off and then on again. Sometimes this doesn't work.

Sometimes playing about with the thermostat batteries makes a difference (no one can figure out why). All in all, it's one of Wintergreen's off-grid mysteries.

This is how the cycle SHOULD work. The heater should be on standby when it is waiting to be called by the thermostat settings (see right). The temperature reflects the temperature in the floor and will vary from what is shown here.

When heat is called for by the thermostat settings, there will be a brief post-purge moment, which will be followed immediately by a pre-purge moment, as pictured:

Pre-purge is followed by ignition, as pictured:

Next is a screen showing 44% firing, and then 100% firing (which later drops to a more efficient level), as indicated in the two pictures below.

If the boiler is talking to the thermostat, there will also be a red light or two lit on the side of the green box, which controls the zones (there are two zones, top light is for the south wing, bottom light is for the north wing). In the picture, the top light (south wing) is on. Note that these red lights come on whenever the thermostat is calling for heat *even if the boiler isn't working.*

When the boiler doesn't work in this fashion, there is an endless loop of post-purge – pre-purge – ignition (fails) – post-purge – pre-purge – ignition (likely fails again) etc., until the boiler has had enough tries. Usually three. Then the error screen comes up and flashes. Press the ENTER RESET button on the right. Flick the switch off and on, and try again. Worst case, you'll do this entire cycle five or six times. And then breathe when it comes on for good (or until the generator kicks in again!). Or pray for summer.

Maintaining the woodstove

The woodstove is a lovely source of heat in the late fall, throughout the winter, and into the early spring. It is, however, a back-up heating source and does not have the capacity to heat the lodge in the coldest months of the year.

The stove is quite straightforward—use paper and kindling to start, and gradually increase the size of logs as the fire takes hold. It burns quite quickly (not air tight), and so it needs quite a bit of constant feeding. Keeping the stove going in the cooler weather also gives the kitchen staff another cooking and warming area.

The only servicing that is required for the woodstove is chimney cleaning every couple of years. We tend to clean the chimney in the odd years (2015, 2017, 2019, etc.)

Water

This section contains three documents, as described below.

How to turn off the water
The water from the well is shut off, occasionally, when the winter weather is fierce and there is no one present in the lodge, or when systems maintenance requires the water to be shut down.

How to turn on the water
This section of the manual describes how to turn on the water if the well has been shut down for maintenance or because of cold weather

Outdoor water
This section describes how to turn the water on and off for the outdoor water source located in the courtyard of the Wintergreen lodge.

Water samples
The final section describes the procedures for ensuring that our drinking water is safe for the public. These procedures include regular water sampling and health inspections.

How to shut off the water

STEP 1: Turn off breaker on electrical panel for continuous flow (tankless) hot water and the breaker for the well: breakers #20 and #22, pictured below and marked with a black sharpie as HWT and WELL, respectively. This means flicking the two switches to the right (the bottom switch, below the well breaker, is permanently set on off). The tankless is in the propane room and is pictured on the right.

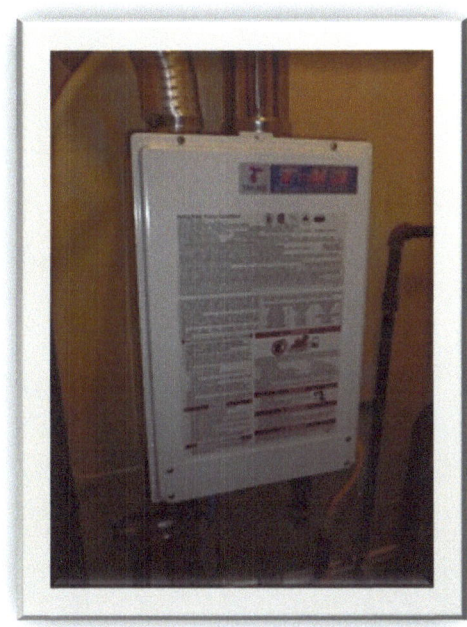

STEP 2: Turn on all faucets (about a third of the way), beginning in the north wing. The hot water is the most important. This means sinks, showers, and bath in staff room –all of them! The only one you won't be able to turn on is the automatic hand-washing faucet.

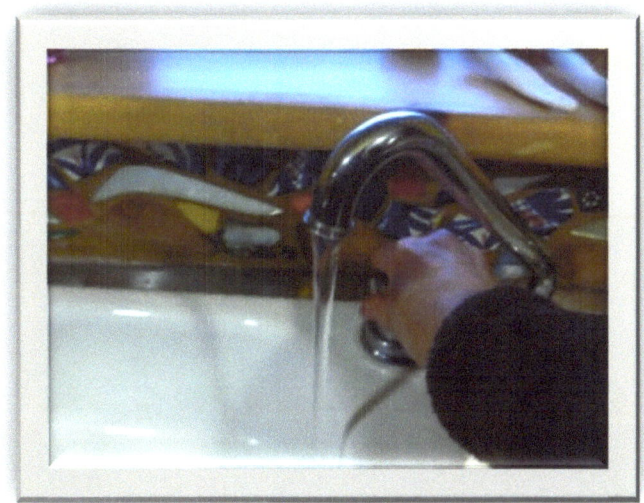

STEP 3: Shut off the flow from the well using the valve at floor level, moving from the position where the valve is parallel to the pipe (open, as pictured on the left) to perpendicular to the pipe (closed, as pictured on the right).

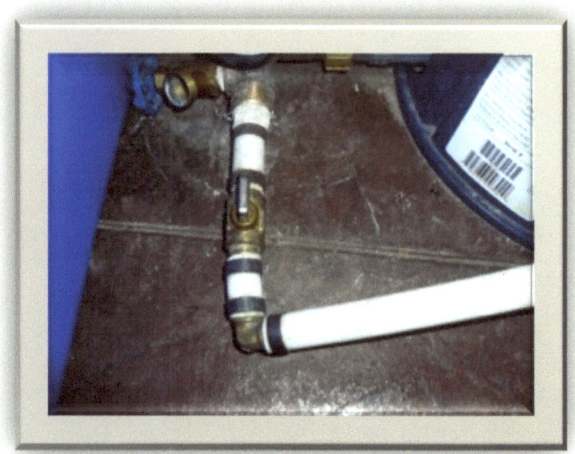 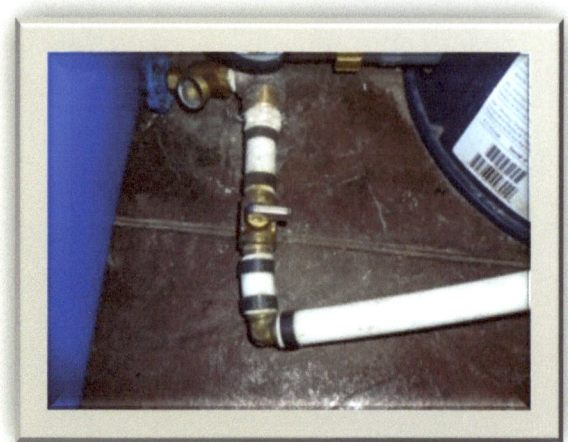

STEP 4: Close off the water to the tankless hot water heater by closing the hot (red) valve and the cold (blue) valves to the perpendicular positions as shown below:

STEP 5: Drain whatever is left in the hot water heater. First open the two grey caps, as pictured. Then open the hot and cold drainage valves (which means they will be parallel to the pipes), and be prepared to catch whatever water comes out. The excess water can go right down the drain in the floor as pictured. Sometimes there will be a bit of a burst coming out of the hot water valve, depending on how much water is still in the tank (shouldn't be very much if the faucets are open: Step 2).

How to turn on the water

STEP 1: Turn off all faucets (chances are, you'll miss one somewhere, and hear a burst of water when the whole system comes on again – be prepared to be startled!)

STEP 2: Close grey caps on tankless hot water. Close drainage valves on tankless hot water (red for hot, blue for cold). Open main valves to the system so that water can once again enter the tankless hot water tank. When you are done with the caps (two) and valves (four – note that some may be "sticky" and require a bit of pressure), the valves and caps should look like the following, with both red and both blue valves pointing "down" and the grey caps closed:

STEP 3: Let the water in again from the well by opening the valve on the floor. This means moving the valve from the position perpendicular to the pipe to a position parallel to the pipe, as shown below:

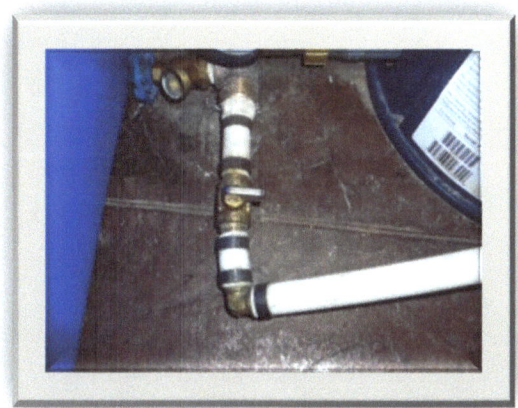 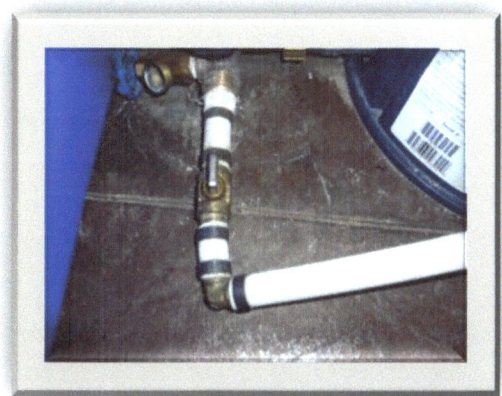

STEP 4: Turn on both the tankless hot water (**HWT #20**) and the well pump (**WELL #22**) by flicking the breaker switches towards the centre (left) as shown. You'll hear a big gush of water as the pump to the well kicks in and restores water to the system. Then you can run out and shut off whatever faucet you might have forgotten to shut off in Step One. And you're done!

NOTE: Sometimes the pipes freeze for the hot water on the North Wing. This is because they're the only ones that aren't tucked into the floor (don't ask!). The hot water pipe runs along the top of the ceiling in the great room. There are holes drilled along the top to ensure that it doesn't freeze, but this system doesn't always work. If there is no hot water in the North Wing, hold a hair dryer (in mechanical room) to the holes and hope for a quick thaw.

Outdoor water

Fall

Outdoor faucet

There is one outdoor faucet, located on the staff-wing side of the courtyard. In the late fall, the water needs to be drained from the pipes that run through the lodge. To do this, first turn off the water source in the mechanical room as pictured below. The picture on the left shows the pipes open; the one on the right is the closed position.

Next, remove the black hose connector from the outdoor faucet. Then turn on the faucet until it drains completely. Leave the faucet open.

Rain barrel

The rain barrel also needs to be disconnected in the fall. Open the faucet near the bottom of the barrel and allow it to drain completely. Leave the faucet open. Remove the barrel from under the downspout and turn on its side for winter storage.

Eaves troughs

The eaves troughs should be cleaned each fall. The ladder is usually behind the sauna. Be sure to have someone holding the ladder when you climb up to clean the troughs.

Spring

Outdoor faucet

The water needs to be re-connected in the spring. To do this, close the outdoor faucet in the courtyard. Then turn on the water source in the mechanical room (see photos on previous page).

Next, hook up the hose to the outdoor faucet. Test the water.

Rain barrel

The rain barrel needs to be reconnected in the spring. Close the faucet near the bottom of the barrel and reposition the rain barrel under the eaves trough downspout. Remove the screening and clean off dead leaves, etc., that may have accumulated over the winter months.

Eaves troughs

The eaves troughs should be cleaned each spring. The ladder is usually behind the sauna. Be sure to have someone holding the ladder when you climb up to clean the troughs.

Water samples

Well water—Small Drinking Water System

Wintergreen's water comes from a well. Because we are considered a "small drinking system" under Regulation 319/08, there are procedures that must be strictly followed.

Small Drinking Water System Number

Our small drinking water system number is **84115KBWv.** This number (case sensitive) appears on the form that accompanies all water samples. The sample bottles and forms are kept in the top drawer next to the washing machine in the office/laundry room.

Public Health Inspections

We are classified as a medium risk seasonal operation. This means that we require two inspection by a Public Health official each year. These inspections usually take place in late-February and late-October. Results of all inspections are kept in a dark blue folder in the office marked "Public Health." The inspection includes kitchen and bathroom safety and cleanliness as well as water.

Water Samples During the Season

A water sample is also taken at the time of inspection. ***Between inspections we must ensure that a water sample is taken every three months.*** Typically, our water samples are submitted quarterly, in March, June, September, and December. Copies of the results of the samples are kept in two locations: in the office at the Wintergreen lodge, and in the corporate document storage at Queen's University.

The water samples that we take are tested by a private laboratory called **Exova,** located at 608 Norris Court in Kingston (phone: 613 634 9307). The samples, once taken, need to be stored in a cooler and then delivered within a few hours to the lab. Results of the testing are emailed to the Executive Director and Operations Manager. Other labs may also be used, including **Paracel Laboratories** and **AGAT Laboratories**, provided that they are added as licensed laboratories to the record.

Water records

There are two binders related to water in the office. There is a red one simply titled "Water," and it contains information about the Well, the Laboratory Services we use, and various items of correspondence regarding the water. It also contains the results of prior testing in a pocket at the back of the binder. The other white and blue one binder, titled, "Drinking Water Systems under the *Health Protection and Promotion Act*" is information provided by the Ministry. The most salient issues for water are marked with yellow tabs in the latter binder, including (a) Notice to Open, (b) Testing, and (c) Notice of Adverse Test Results and Issue Resolution.

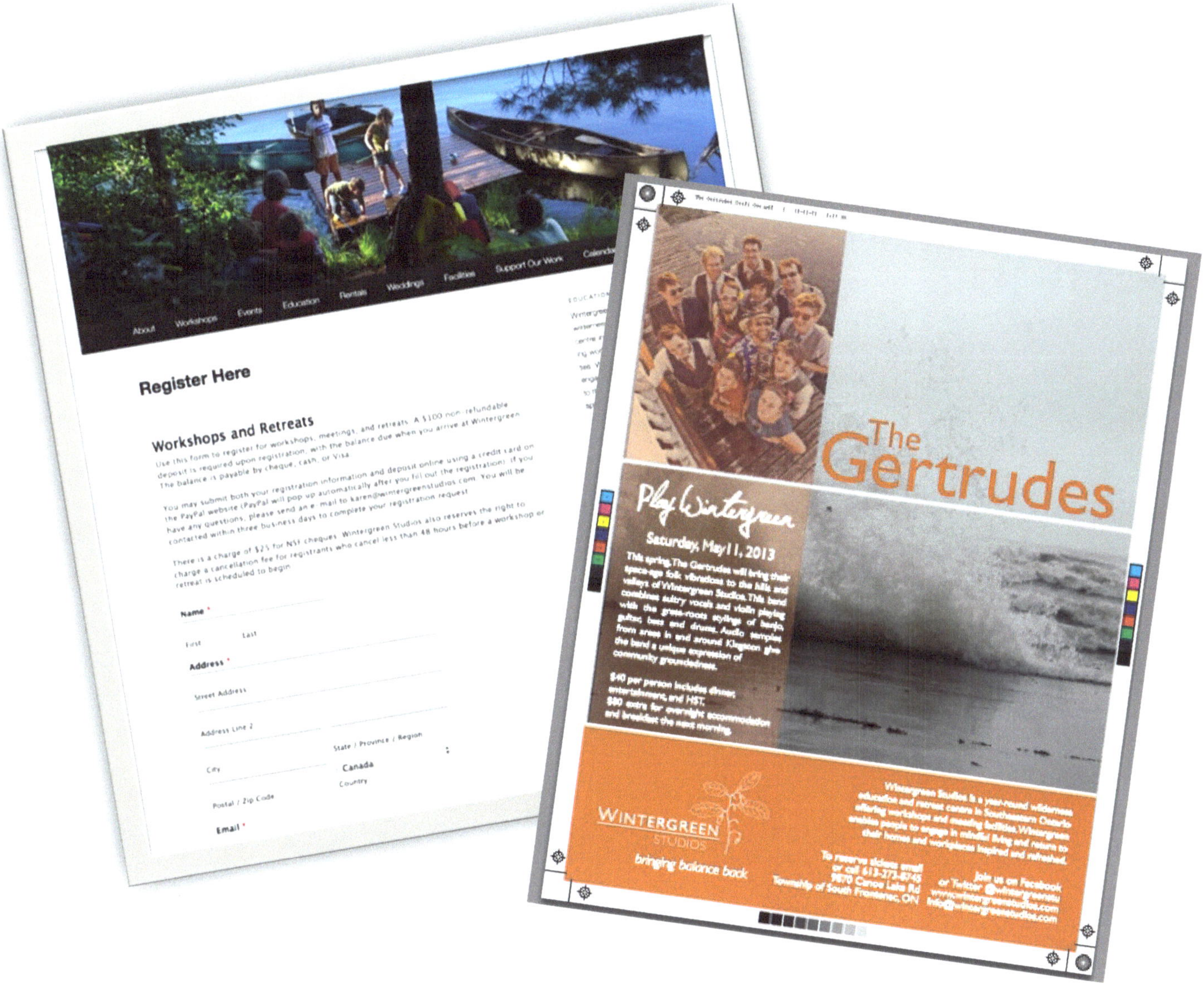

Human Resources, Programs, and Finance Handbook

2016–2018

If you can't go where people are happier, try to make people happier where you are.

– *Ashleigh Brilliant*

Ideas without action are useless.

– *Harvey Mackay*

I long to accomplish a great and noble task, but it is my chief duty to accomplish small tasks as if they were great and noble.

– *Helen Keller*

Introduction to Human Resources, Programs, and Finance

This manual contains procedures and protocols for human resources, program administration, and finance.

General topics that are included are roles and responsibilities of employees, staff, and Board volunteers, including job descriptions where appropriate to do so. Protocols for registering guests and operating events are also described. The operations of Wintergreen Studios Press are detailed. Our privacy statement is included, and processes for invoicing and receipting, tracking systems, and registration forms are also contained in this manual.

The appendices include various sample forms for registration, financial reporting, invoicing, and receipting Wintergreen's partners and guests.

Human Resources
Overview

The people who make Wintergreen work are comprised of volunteers (including the Board of Directors and Executive Director and occasional student interns), permanent part-time staff, and contract staff.

Permanent contract staff, and in some instances, contract staff and student interns, are selected by the Human Resource Committee of the Board of Directors. In most cases, contract staff are selected by the Operations Manager and Executive Director.

Permanent part-time staff have job descriptions and are paid benefits according to provincial laws. They receive ongoing informal feedback from the Executive Director and a more formal evaluation in the fall of each year. Job descriptions for the three permanent part-time staff, namely, the Operations Manager, the Facilities Manager, and the Marketing and Communications Director, are attached. A description for the Education and Outreach Coordinator is also attached, and this position is filled when funds are available.

Permanent part-time staff are paid on a monthly basis by Wintergreen's accountant. They receive monthly pay stubs and an electronic transfer is made directly to their bank accounts.

Contract staff are paid as invoiced, by cheques made out by the Executive Director. Contract staff are paid on a negotiated hourly rate, depending on the tasks performed and on the expertise of the contracted staff. Typically, kitchen staff and casual labour receive $12.00/hr. Carpenters are generally paid between $25.00 and $30.00 an hour. The bookkeeper is paid $25.00/hr. Student labour rates are $12.00/hr.

The organizational structure of Wintergreen is represented on the figure that appears on the following page.

Organization Chart

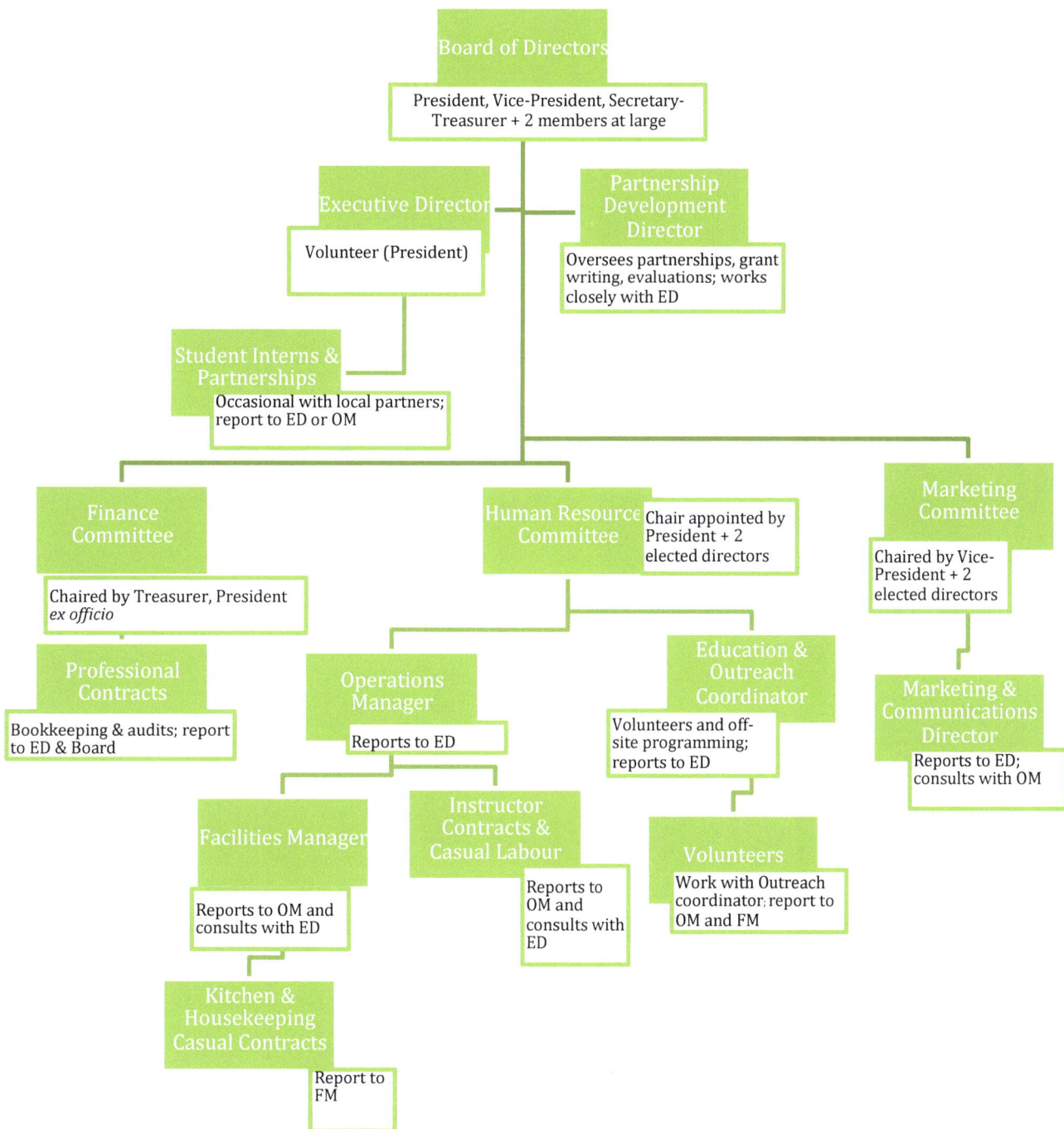

Board Committees

Finance Committee

Chair: Secretary-Treasurer

Members: President, Partnership Development Officer

Meeting Schedule: Generally in August before the September Board Meeting and AGM

The Finance Committee is responsible for:

- ✓ Developing the Annual Budget
- ✓ Vetting and approving the Year-end Financial Statements
- ✓ Providing recommendations to the Board for any acquisitions or expenditures outside the approved budget
- ✓ Setting policies for travel
- ✓ Setting policies for signing authority

Job Descriptions: Permanent Part-Time and Casual Employees

Executive Director

Position: Executive Director **Incumbent:** Rena Upitis (VOLUNTEER)

Department: Board of Directors **Date:** April 10, 2007

GENERAL ACCOUNTABILITY

Reporting to the Board of Directors through the President, the incumbent provides overall management and leadership in implementing Board policy in a manner consistent with the mission and goals of Wintergreen Studios and its affiliated programs and partners.

COMPENSATION

Currently a .75 FTE volunteer position

$65,000–75,000/yr + benefits p.a., commensurate with experience

NATURE AND SCOPE

Wintergreen Studios is an education and retreat centre where writers, artists, and craftspeople offer short courses in the fine and domestic arts. Participants learn new skills, engage in mindful living, and return to their homes and workplaces refreshed and inspired to live more lightly.

Wintergreen Studios meets this goal by:

1. offering a variety of short courses and programs in the literary arts and fine arts

2. providing facilities for small meetings, program orientations, and individual and group retreats—gatherings where an inspiring setting can help a group meet its vision.

3. supporting research on the role of the arts and the natural environment in enhancing wellness and quality of life.

KEY RESPONSIBILITIES

Implement board policy and decisions
- Act as a resource to Board of Directors so that policy decisions are made on an informed basis
- Gather, interpret and articulate information to Board about community trends and resources as they relate to enhancing the Board's capacity for effective communication, decision-making and long-term planning
- Keep Board informed (on a timely basis) of significant issues affecting the development and delivery of programs and services
- Oversee development and implementation of orientation for incoming Board Members
- Provide guidance and advice to Board on process issues such as establishing and interpreting terms of reference, decision-making and accountability
- Attend and participate in meetings, assisting with materials and recording note/minutes for distribution as required

Monitor and oversee financial management of the organization
- Ensure development of annual budget and present to Treasurer for evaluation and modification as required
- Strategic Plan development, updating and monitoring
- Identify, prioritize and provide advice and counsel to aid Board in accessing potential fund-raising alternatives
- Maintain relationships with funding sources and prepare funding proposals

Manage the staff
- Ensure appropriate staffing consistent with needs of Wintergreen's constituents and within the constraints of the organization's physical and financial resources
- Develop and maintain the Manuals, Handbooks and Kits for operations and policies
- Develop and maintain appropriate job descriptions for all staff
- Orient and train staff
- Evaluate staff
- Ensure staff are appropriately compensated

Maintain, acquire and dispose of physical assets
- Ensure that facilities, furniture and equipment are appropriate to needs of the organization
- Provide recommendations to the Board for any acquisitions or expenditures that are outside the approved budget
- Ensure proper maintenance of facilities, furniture and equipment
- As necessary, dispose of outdated or worn out equipment

Develop, plan and deliver programs and services
- Monitor community needs on an ongoing basis
- Develop programs and services consistent with community needs

- Monitor programs and services to ensure consistency with criteria established by funding sources and the mission and goals of the organization
- Annually prepare and provide to the Board, and other applicable bodies, summary reports of programs and services, including recommendations for future improvement and change
- Regularly obtain statistical and qualitative feedback about program and service delivery
- Guide marketing and communications activities
- Provide consultative services on bylaws, procedures, conflict management
- Monitor staff benefits and property insurance programs

Establish, maintain and advance community relations
- Initiate and develop relationships with a broad range of community sectors
- Undertake activities within the community that enhance the visibility of the organization
- Represent the organization on appropriate committees, networks, and joint projects
- Develop and provide information about the organization's goals, programs and services

QUALIFICATIONS

Essential Qualifications

- An advanced university degree, preferably in education or administration
- Experience in managing a community-based not-for-profit organization
- Proficient in using information technology
- Exemplary written and oral communication skills
- Experience in initiating, planning, implementing, and evaluating programs and services
- Experience in staff management

Qualifications Considered An Asset

- Demonstrated ability to merge education, business, and adult education principles
- Awareness of trends and development in holistic and informal learning
- Exceptional negotiation and communication skills
- Ability to work with high caliber faculty to create exceptional educational experiences
- In alignment with Wintergreen's vision, goals and core values
- Ability to present, develop, and implement new ideas
- Ability to work independently
- Organizational skills
- Team player

Operations and Facilities Manager

Position: Operations and Facilities Manager **Incumbent:** Diane Black

Department: Human Resources **Date:** November 30, 2015

GENERAL ACCOUNTABILITY

Reporting to the Human Resource Committee and the Executive Director, the Operations and Facilities Manager is accountable for organizing and supporting all events (workshops, retreats, conferences, open houses), and plays a role in guiding the development of the retreats, meetings, and course offerings at Wintergreen.

The Events Manager is responsible for arranging contracts and needs of instructors, rental arrangements, participant registration, accommodation and meals, and for other related general administration. The Operations and Facilities Manager is *not responsible for the physical plant* of Wintergreen except to oversee general kitchen and lodge maintenance as associated with the events.

COMPENSATION

$1200/month for 8 days distributed as required + benefits (.35 FTE)

$36,000 - $48,000+ benefits p.a., commensurate with experience

NATURE AND SCOPE

Wintergreen Studios is an education and retreat centre where writers, artists, and craftspeople offer short courses in the fine and domestic arts. Participants learn new skills, engage in mindful living, and return to their homes and workplaces refreshed and inspired to live more lightly.

Wintergreen Studios meets this goal by:

1. offering a variety of short courses and programs in the literary arts and fine arts

2. providing facilities for small meetings, program orientations, and individual and group retreats—gatherings where an inspiring setting can help a group meet its vision.

3. supporting research on the role of the arts and the natural environment in enhancing wellness and quality of life.

KEY RESPONSIBILITIES

1. **General Administration**
   Administering workshops and events including, but not limited to:
   - course registrations (WuFoo registration and Google docs)
   - communications with participants by phone and internet with all issues that arise including payment, dietary needs, accommodation, cancellations, waitlists
   - pre-workshop communication letter
   - staffing each event as required with casual employees, contracted help, and volunteers (see below re: meal planning)
   - post-workshop follow up
   - contributing to marketing as required (e.g., postering)
   - preparing receipts and invoices as required
   - managing contracts (see below)
   - Submit water samples as needed by the Province of Ontario
   - Coordinate Health inspections (spring and fall)

2. **Managing Contracts**
   Setting up contracts and/or memoranda for workshop instructors and retreat coordinators, as well as:
   - Checking in with instructors regarding workshop numbers and reminding instructors to market through their own channels
   - Serving as a liaison between staff, contract employees, and board administration

3. **Workshop meal planning and oversight**
   Planning meals and providing guest accommodations:
   - Ensure the lodge is "event ready" on the day of an event, workshop, open house, or inspection (see Operations Manual)
   - Plan menu taking into account seasonal offerings
   - Purchase ingredients and supplies
   - Prepare and serve meals as Lead Chef or assign a Lead Chef and make recipes, instructions and ingredients available to the kitchen staff in your absence
   - Ensure food is prepared in accordance with health & hygiene regulations
   - Awareness of suitability of ingredients to different groups, e.g., vegan, celiac
   - Maintain a clean and tidy kitchen pre and post events (includes removal of all recycling and trash directly after a workshop)
   - Report any problems encountered to the Executive Director
   - Provide a high standard of cleanliness and order in the kitchen and refrigerator (includes dusting all open surfaces and window sills, etc.)
   - Launder tea towels and wash rags
   - Sweep and wash kitchen floors before and after events
   - General tear down after events as described in the Operational Manual

4. **Staffing**
   Staffing for all workshops and events (includes volunteers), including:
   - Identifying staff for each event and noting on the Google doc staffing document
   - Overseeing facilities and kitchen during events
   - Helping with onsite workshops as required (cooking, cleaning, troubleshooting with participants, etc.)

QUALIFICATIONS

Essential Qualifications

- A university degree, preferably in education or administration
- Experience or training in all of the following areas:
   - Culinary arts
   - Website Design/Management
   - Management of staff

Qualifications Considered An Asset

- Awareness of trends and development in holistic and informal learning
- Understanding of the content of Wintergreen's workshops
- Exceptional negotiation and communication skills
- Strong written and oral communication skills
- Understanding of marketing and communications to adult learners
- Ability to work with faculty to create exceptional educational experiences
- In alignment with Wintergreen's vision, goals and core values
- Ability to present, develop, and implement new ideas
- Ability to work independently
- Organizational skills
- Team player

SUPERVISION

Received

The Operations and Facilities Manager works closely with the Executive Director to determine how the aims and objectives of Wintergreen will be met through its programs and services.

Exercised

Supervision of professional contracts, instructors and housekeeping, and kitchen staff, including paid and volunteer staff.

Operations Manager

Position: Operations Manager

Department: Human Resources

Incumbent: Karen Smereka

Date: Dec 1, 2010 - November 30, 2015

GENERAL ACCOUNTABILITY

Reporting to the Human Resource Committee and the Executive Director, the incumbent is accountable for assisting in the provision of the full range of services and programs of Wintergreen, and will play a role in guiding the development of the retreats, meetings, and course offerings at Wintergreen.

The Operations Manager is responsible for arranging details for instructors, classes, workshops, event planners, and other clients at Wintergreen Studios; and for general administration.

COMPENSATION

$1200/month for 8 days distributed as required + benefits (currently .35 FTE)

$36,000 - $48,000+ benefits p.a., commensurate with experience

NATURE AND SCOPE

Wintergreen Studios is an education and retreat centre where writers, artists, and craftspeople offer short courses in the fine and domestic arts. Participants learn new skills, engage in mindful living, and return to their homes and workplaces refreshed and inspired to live more lightly.

Wintergreen Studios meets this goal by:

1. offering a variety of short courses and programs in the literary arts and fine arts

2. providing facilities for small meetings, program orientations, and individual and group retreats—gatherings where an inspiring setting can help a group meet its vision.

3. supporting research on the role of the arts and the natural environment in enhancing wellness and quality of life.

KEY RESPONSIBILITIES

1. **Programming**
   - Administering workshops and events including, but not limited to:
     - course registrations
     - communications with participants by phone and internet
     - costing out supplies and other items
     - contributing to marketing and communications functions as required
     - preparing receipts, invoices, etc., for participants and bookkeeper
     - organizing trade show attendance
     - helping to prepare press releases and other media tools
     - managing contracts (see below)

2. **Overseeing Contracts**
   - Setting up contracts, job descriptions, and memoranda of agreement, as required, for professional services, website maintenance and/or design, student interns, workshop instructors, and housekeeping, physical plant, and kitchen staff
   - Serving as a liaison between staff, contract employees, and board administration

QUALIFICATIONS

Essential Qualifications

- A university degree, preferably in education or administration
- Experience or training in all of the following areas:
  - Curriculum Development
  - Presentation Delivery
  - Website Design/Management
  - Management of staff

Qualifications Considered An Asset

- Demonstrated ability to merge education, business, and adult education principles
- Awareness of trends and development in holistic and informal learning
- Understanding of the content of Wintergreen's workshops
- Exceptional negotiation and communication skills
- Strong written and oral communication skills
- Understanding of marketing and communications to adult learners
- Ability to work with faculty to create exceptional educational experiences
- In alignment with Wintergreen's vision, goals and core values
- Ability to present, develop, and implement new ideas
- Ability to work independently
- Organizational skills
- Team player

SUPERVISION

Received

The Operations Manager works closely with the Executive Director to determine how the aims and objectives of Wintergreen will be met through its programs and services.

S/he consults regularly with the Executive Director as well as the Director of Marketing and Communications and Facilities Manager.

Exercised

Supervision of professional contracts, student interns, instructors and housekeeping, physical plant, and kitchen staff, including paid and volunteer staff.

Responsibilities include designing job descriptions, selection of coordinators, monitoring and evaluation.

Facilities Manager

Position: Facilities Manager

Department: Human Resources

Incumbent: Louise Cooper

Date: Oct 1, 2012 – Nov 30, 2015

GENERAL ACCOUNTABILITY

Reporting to the Operations Manager, the incumbent is accountable for overseeing, planning and preparing a full range of services and duties to ensure the highest degree of comfort and enjoyment for participants participating in weekend retreats and workshops at Wintergreen Studios.

The Facilities Manager is responsible for planning and preparing meals and for ensuring that a high standard of cleanliness and order is at Wintergreen Studios. The Facilities Manager also oversees the off-grid systems (solar hot water, fuel levels, battery levels, etc.) as required.

COMPENSATION

$750/month for 6.25 days as required (currently .27 FTE)

$30,000 - $38,000 + benefits p.a., commensurate with experience

KEY RESPONSIBILITIES

Kitchen
- Plan menu in consultation with Operations Manager and/or Executive Director
- Plan, plant, cultivate, and harvest Wintergreen's herb and vegetable gardens
- Purchase all ingredients and supplies
- Prepare and serve meals as the Lead Cook
- Ensure food is prepared in accordance with health & hygiene regulations
- Awareness of suitability of ingredients to different groups, i.e., vegetarian, gluten free, vegan, & kosher
- Maintain a clean and tidy kitchen
- Report any problems encountered to the Operations Manager

Housekeeping
- Provide a high standard of cleanliness and order at Wintergreen
- Ensure that the exterior approach to Wintergreen is free of obstruction and attractive to guests. Lawns should be mowed prior to events; arrange to have perennials weeded as required.
- Check cleanliness and prepare rooms before arrival of guests. Ensure all guests have towels, flowers, Wintergreen postcards, and chocolates.

- Clean bathrooms twice a day while guests are in the lodge, and ensure that towels and toilette paper is regularly replenished
- Ensure that corridors and great room are clean and clear of obstructions
- Maintain a friendly and approachable attitude toward guests and coworkers
- Launder sheets and towels at the end of the workshop and re-make beds
- Sweep or wash or vacuum floors as required
- Solve housekeeping or maintenance issues as required
- Report any deficiencies or problems to the Operations Manager
- Label and submit all lost and found items to the Operations Manager

QUALIFICATIONS
- Excellent communication and interpersonal skills
- Previous kitchen experience cooking for groups of up to 20 people
- Ability to work under pressure
- Organised
- Motivated and enthusiastic

SUPERVISION

The Facilities Manager works with the Operations Manager on workshop details and menus and supervises any support casual kitchen and housekeeping staff.

Marketing and Communications Director

Position: Director of Marketing & Communications   **Incumbent:** Claire Grady-Smith

Department: Marketing   **Date:** Jan 1, 2012 – June, 2013

GENERAL ACCOUNTABILITY

Reporting to the Marketing Committee and to the Executive Director, the incumbent will play a leadership role in guiding the development of the marketing and communications activities for Wintergreen Studios and Wintergreen Studios Press.

The Director of Marketing and Communications is responsible for researching, developing, and actualizing a marketing and communications plan; chairing Steering Committees for major fund-raising events; developing social media, general networking, administrative structures related to marketing and communications. S/he is also accountable for assisting in the overall provision of the full range of services, programs, and products for Wintergreen Studios and Wintergreen Studios Press.

COMPENSATION

$1500/month for 8 days as required (currently .35 FTE) until June 30, 2012. *July 1, 2013–June 30, 2014 will be on a contract basis.*

$42,000 - $52,000 + benefits p.a., commensurate with experience

NATURE AND SCOPE

Wintergreen's mission is to enable people to develop literary, artistic, and domestic skills and to be engaged in mindful and sustainable living, so that when they return to their homes and workplaces, they are both inspired and refreshed.

To enact this mission, Wintergreen offers three streams of activities: workshops, meetings and retreats, and research in ecology and the arts. Workshops are in the areas of the literary arts, creative and fine arts, and sustainable building. Meeting and retreat spaces are available to groups interested in sustainable technologies and the natural environment. The research stream includes projects with teachers and artist-educators involved in school activities focusing on environmental issues through the arts.

KEY RESPONSIBILITIES

The position involves research, strategic analysis, planning, and actualizing the marketing activities in five general areas:

1. analyzing the target markets as follows:
    a. past and potential course participants
    b. past and potential retreat and group meeting audiences

      c. potential volunteers (time, ideas)
      d. increasing the donor base
      e. supporting readership of WSP books
2. developing internet-based marketing strategies
3. developing, designing, and producing print-based promotional materials for workshops, readings, retreats and book titles
4. leading Steering Committees for a major fund-raising events, including corporate sponsorship and community involvement
5. serving as a member of the Marketing Committee.

The incumbent understands the overall operations of Wintergreen, including the day-to-day operations and the technical aspects of operating the off-grid facility.

QUALIFICATIONS

Essential Qualifications

- A university degree, preferably in business with an emphasis on marketing
- Experience and/or training in all of the following areas:
  - Marketing
  - Fundraising and Development
  - Website Design/Management
  - Web-based marketing campaigns

Additional Qualifications

- strong communication skills, both oral and written
- technological savvy
- an abiding interest in the arts and the environment
- ability to work independently, taking into account the advice of supervisors
- understanding of small business and charitable organizations
- understanding of the content of Wintergreen's workshops

SUPERVISION

Received

The Director of Marketing and Communications works closely with the Board of Directors to determine how the aims and objectives of Wintergreen will be met through its programs and services. S/he reports directly to the President and Vice-President of Wintergreen (the Vice-President chairs the Marketing Committee).

Exercised

Supervision of student interns and volunteer staff. Responsibilities include designing marketing strategies, and monitoring and evaluation of same.

Education and Outreach Coordinator

Position: Education and Outreach Coordinator **Incumbent:** Karen Smereka

Department: Human Resources **Date:** April 1, 2013 – Nov 30, 2015

GENERAL ACCOUNTABILITY

Reporting to the Human Resource Committee, the incumbent is accountable for assisting in the provision of the full range of sustainability programs and educational resources related to Wintergreen's environmental education programs.

COMPENSATION

$400/month distributed as required + benefits (currently .15 FTE)

$32,000 - $40,000 + benefits p.a., commensurate with experience

NATURE AND SCOPE

Wintergreen Studios is an education and retreat centre where artists and craftspeople offer short courses in the fine and domestic arts. Participants learn new skills, engage in mindful living, and return to their homes and workplaces refreshed and inspired to live more lightly.

Wintergreen Studios meets this goal by:

1. offering a variety of short courses and programs in the domestic and fine arts
2. providing facilities for small meetings, program orientations, and retreats—gatherings where an inspiring setting can help a group meet its vision.
3. supporting research on the role of the arts and the natural environment in enhancing wellness and quality of life.

KEY RESPONSIBILITIES

1. **Programming**
   - Designing workshops and events in sustainability including, but not limited to:
     - Workshops & Courses
     - Sustainability Tours
     - Off-site seminars
     - Online materials

2. **Outreach: Overseeing Volunteers and Cultivating Partnerships**
   - Setting up meetings, networks, schedules, memoranda of agreement, incentives, evaluation procedures, etc., as required for student interns, workshop instructors, volunteers, and partners
   - Serving as a liaison between staff, community partners, students, and the Board

QUALIFICATIONS

Essential Qualifications

- A university degree, preferably in environmental education or the biological sciences
- Experience or training in all of the following areas:
    - First Aid
    - Curriculum Development
    - Presentation Delivery
    - Website Design/Management

Qualifications Considered An Asset

- Demonstrated ability to merge education and adult education principles
- Ability to create high quality workshops for face-to-face and online delivery
- Awareness of trends and development in holistic and informal learning
- Understanding of the content of Wintergreen's workshops
- Exceptional negotiation and communication skills
- Strong written and oral communication skills
- Understanding of marketing and communications to adult learners
- Ability to work with high caliber faculty to create exceptional educational experiences
- In alignment with Wintergreen's vision, goals and core values
- Ability to present, develop, and implement new ideas
- Ability to work independently
- Organizational skills
- Ability to multitask
- Team player

SUPERVISION

Received

The Education and Outreach Coordinator works closely with the Operations Manager, and the Executive Director to determine how the aims and objectives of Wintergreen will be met through its environmental programs and services. The Education and Outreach Coordinator consults regularly with the Director of Marketing and Communications.

Exercised

Supervision of student interns and instructors, including paid and volunteer staff.

Job Descriptions: Casual Contracts

Bookkeeper

Position: Bookkeeper
Department: Finance

Incumbent: Donna Poirier
Date: February 9, 2011

GENERAL ACCOUNTABILITY

Reporting to the Finance Committee, the incumbent is accountable for providing month-to-month bookkeeping and basic accounting requirements for Wintergreen Studios, Inc. The Bookkeeper operates with limited supervision for routine work and is able to identify when direction is required.

NATURE AND SCOPE

Wintergreen Studios is an education and retreat centre where artists and craftspeople offer short courses in the fine and domestic arts. Participants learn new skills, engage in mindful living, and return to their homes and workplaces inspired and refreshed.

Wintergreen Studios will meet this goal by:

1. offering a variety of short courses and programs in the domestic and fine arts

2. providing facilities that may be used for small meetings, program orientations, and individual and group retreats—gatherings where an inspiring setting can help a group meet its vision.

3. supporting research on the role of the arts and the natural environment in enhancing wellness and quality of life.

KEY RESPONSIBILITIES

1. **General Accounting**
   - Set up Wintergreen's books and secure back-up copies
   - Prepare monthly balance and income statements
   - File information return for charitable organization annually
   - Coordinate annual year-end statements with Collins Blay

2. **Pay Roll**
   - Keep records of contracts for services and employment contracts including contracts, SIN #s, payment details, etc.
   - Issue T4 forms for employees as required

3. **Accounts Payable**

    - File for HST rebates

4. **Other Duties as Assigned**

QUALIFICATIONS

Essential Qualifications

- Fundamental understanding of all facets of accounting
- Proficiency in several computerized bookkeeping systems
- Experienced in keeping books for other charitable organizations

Qualifications Considered An Asset

- Excellent organization, time-management, administrative, and computer skills
- Strong written and oral communication skills
- Attention to detail
- In alignment with Wintergreen's vision, goals and core values
- Interpersonal Skills
- Ability to work independently
- Team player

SUPERVISION

Received

The Bookkeeper works with the Board of Directors to determine how the aims and objectives of Wintergreen will be met through its programs and services. S/he consults with the Treasurer and CEO as necessary.

The Bookkeeper consults with senior managers at Collins Blay & Co for advice as required.

Kitchen and Housekeeping Assistant

Position: Kitchen & Housekeeping Assistant   **Incumbent:** Varies

Department: Kitchen & Housekeeping   **Date:** Seasonal/Casual

---

GENERAL ACCOUNTABILITY
Reporting to the Facilities Manager, the incumbent is accountable for assisting with a full range of services and duties to ensure the highest degree of comfort and enjoyment for participants participating in weekend retreats and workshops at Wintergreen Studios. *This is an occasional contract position, not permanent employment.*

The Kitchen and Housekeeping Assistant is responsible for assisting in the preparation and serving of meals and for ensuring that a high standard of cleanliness and order is maintained at Wintergreen Studios. The Kitchen and Housekeeping Assistant should become familiar with the Operations Manuals relevant to his/her work.

COMPENSATION
$ 12.00/hr., payable upon receipt of invoice made out to Wintergreen Studios. Travel time can be claimed if the contract staff lives more than 30 minutes from Wintergreen.

KEY RESPONSIBILITIES
Kitchen
- Prepare and serve meals under the supervision of the Facilities Manager
- Ensure food is prepared in accordance with health & hygiene regulations
- Awareness of suitability of ingredients to different groups, i.e., vegetarian, gluten free, vegan, kosher.
- Maintain a clean and tidy kitchen
- Perform regular cleaning functions as instructed by the Facilities Manager, such as recycling and composting
- Report any problems encountered to the Facilities Manager

Housekeeping
- Provide a high standard of cleanliness and order at Wintergreen
- Clean bathrooms and ensure that towels and toilette paper is regularly replenished as instructed by the Facilities Manager
- Ensure that corridors and great room are clean and free of obstructions
- Maintain a friendly and approachable attitude toward guests and coworkers
- Launder sheets and towels on the last day of the workshop and make-up beds
- Report any deficiencies or problems to the Facilities Manager
- Label and submit all lost and found items to the Facilities Manager

QUALIFICATIONS
- Excellent communication and interpersonal skills
- Previous kitchen experience cooking for groups of up to 20
- Ability to work under pressure
- Organised
- Motivated and enthusiastic

SUPERVISION

The Kitchen and Housekeeping Assistant works with the Facilities Manager and the Operations Manager and reports to the Facilities Manager directly.

Registration and Event Planning

Overview

The Operations Manager oversees registration for all Wintergreen workshops, events, and retreats. In consultation with the Executive Director and Facilities Manager, the Operations Manager coordinates the availability of space and programs, ensures that appropriate accommodations are available for overnight guests, oversees menus in terms of dietary restrictions, and manages other operations pertaining to Wintergreen's programming.

There are procedures in place for signing up for workshops, events, and retreats, and nearly all of Wintergreen's registration occurs online. However, for some on-off events or partnership events, registration still takes place using telephone, email, and surface mail.

The Operations Manager records all information for each event on a separate "Google doc," which is made available to the event organizer, if applicable, as well as to the Facilities Manager and Executive Director. Both the Facilities Manager and Executive Director have editing privileges on the "Google docs" so that these documents become live for all staff involved.

The Operations Manager also oversees the staffing for Wintergreen, ensuring that there are enough contract staff and volunteers at each event for things to run smoothly. This can be a delicate dance; while we want to ensure that staff can perform their duties with ease and enjoyment, we also need to balance costs so that events operate at least on a break-even basis.

Checklists for registration and planning for each type of event appear on the following pages. These include (a) workshops, (b) dinner-entertainment evenings, (c) private cabin retreats, and (d) group retreats. Checklists for off-site workshops and tours are currently being developed.

Workshops

Upon receiving the workshop dates, instructor information, and description from the ED or the Programs Committee, the Operations and Facilities Manager does the following:

- ☐ List the event on the Wintergreen calendar.

- ☐ Check that the workshop is clearly described on the website and that the description is free of errors.

- ☐ Ensure that the instructor is pleased with the workshop description.

- ☐ Negotiate a contract with the instructor, based on information provided by the Executive Director. Honoraria vary from one workshop to another. Travel is reimbursed at the rate of $.42/km.

- ☐ Begin a "Google doc" in wintergreenstudios99@gmail.com with columns for participant names, contact information, accommodation type, fee, deposit, dietary restrictions, and any other pertinent information.

- ☐ Monitor registrations, which could come as online notifications (through WuFoo) or direct inquiries by telephone, email, or surface mail.

- ☐ Ongoing communication with participants and instructorsregarding their needs and managing expectations.

- ☐ Keep a waiting list for workshops that are over-subscribed. Notify people on the waiting list if a place becomes available.

- ☐ Alert the Executive Director if registrations are low, so that more direct marketing can be put in place or the workshop can be postponed or cancelled in a timely manner.

- ☐ Determine the number of staff required as the workshop approaches.

- ☐ Send pre-workshop homework to participants as required.

- ☐ Plan menu and circulate for comment.

- ☐ Send letter to participants, with a copy to the instructor(s), a week before the workshop is scheduled to begin (see sample letter in Appendix).

- ☐ Post workshop communication, including critical feedback, photographic releases, testimonials, lost items, supporting ongoing learning arising out of the workshop, and sharing photographs.

Dinner-Entertainment Events and One Day Gatherings

Upon receiving the date for an event or gathering, information about musicians/artists/facilitators, and the event description from the ED or the Programs Committee, the Operations and Facilities Manager does the following:

- ❏ Check that the event is clearly described on the website, noted on the calendar, and that the description is free of errors.

- ❏ Begin a "Google doc" in wintergreenstudios99@gmail.com with columns for participant names, contact information, accommodation type, fee, deposit, dietary restrictions, and any other pertinent information.

- ❏ Create contract for performer/group.

- ❏ Ensure that the musicians/writers/presenters are pleased with the event description.

- ❏ Check that the date is correctly listed on the Wintergreen website calendar.

- ❏ Plan accommodations and meals as required.

Weddings and Other Group Retreats

Upon receiving the dates for a wedding or retreat and the event description from the Executive Director, the Operations Manager does the following:

- ❏ List the retreat on the Wintergreen calendar.

- ❏ Check that the event is clearly described on the website and that the description is free of errors.

- ❏ Prepare contract with details regarding expectations and payment schedule.

- ❏ Begin a "Google doc" on wintergreenstudios99@gmail.com with columns for participant names, contact information, accommodation type, fee, deposit, dietary restrictions, and any other pertinent information.

- ❏ Ensure that the event coordinators are pleased with the event description.

- ❏ Check that the dates are correctly listed on the Wintergreen website calendar. For any changes that need to be made, contact the Executive Director (web mistress).

- ❏ Meal planning and accommodation needs.

- ❏ Manage invoices and receipts.

- ❏ Ongoing communication with group prior to retreat.

Private Cabin Retreats

Wintergreen offers two types of several cabins for private retreats – the Parthenon, Hobbit House, and Beach House, as well as Paddy's Lake Cabin in special circumstances.

Upon receiving a request for a private retreat (usually from the online form or through a telephone or email request), the Operations and Facilities Manager does the following:

- ❑ Check that the dates are available on the Wintergreen calendar.
- ❑ Add information to the "Google doc" for private retreats.
- ❑ List the retreat on the Wintergreen calendar.
- ❑ Communicate with Grounds Keeper and/or Executive Director regarding readiness of the cabins and indicate whether the guests need to be met and guided to the cabin site.
- ❑ Answer guests' questions via email prior to their stay.
- ❑ Ensure payment is received in advance and sent receipt.
- ❑ Post-retreat communication and tasks (e.g., testimonials, lost items, etc.)

Book Publishing: Wintergreen Studios Press

One of the activities of Wintergreen Studios is a publishing arm, specializing in literary works and books dealing generally with education, culture, and the environment (see www.wintergreenstudiospress.com). Over the past several years, Wintergreen Studios Press has published over a dozen books. While it is anticipated that this part of Wintergreen's operations will diminish over the next five to ten years, the publishing arm will remain active, particularly for books that support our educational initiatives.

Governance and History

For the early part of the work of WSP, the Executive Director of Wintergreen, guided by a four-person volunteer Advisory Board, took care of all matters dealing with publication. In 2012, a Marketing and Communications Director was hired. Eight months after that contract was created a broader position was developed so that the current Marketing and Communications Director has responsibilities not only for the Press, but also for Wintergreen Studios as a whole.

Because the operations for book publishing were being simplified as the 2013–2014 Operations Manuals were being written, we have document here the best practices for book publication. Other aspects of Wintergreen's Marketing Plan appear in the next section. This Marketing Plan will be reviewed and modified during the 2013–2014 year.

Book Publication Protocols

All prospective authors send materials directly to the Acquisitions Editor for WSP, following the procedures listed on the WSP website. All manuscripts are discussed at monthly Advisory Board meetings, and a rejection list is kept as a "Google doc" and is available to Advisory Board members and to the Marketing and Communications Director.

For books that are deemed worthy of a full read, authors are notified and asked to send an electronic manuscript. Full manuscripts are read by at least two Board members, and, pending a positive outcome, are sent for full review.

For manuscripts accepted by the Press, one of the Board members creates the book design. Copy-editing is done in-house unless there is additional funding in place, in which case a contract for copy-editing is created and signed. The Press works closely with authors in customizing the publication and uses *CreateSpace*, a branch of Amazon, to create books on a print-on-demand basis.

Once a book title has been through the extensive review, design, editing, and pre-publication phase, marketing for the title begins. The marketing protocol appears in the following section.

Four publications a year is our maximum possible for our available financial and human resources. Publication dates are established for Saturdays. In years when four books are published, two are published in the spring (April and May) and two are published in the fall (October and November). The spring and fall publications are normally a month apart to allow for publicity and launch planning. Once a year, books are delivered to Kingston, Ottawa and Toronto libraries.

Marketing

Five weeks prior to pub date:
Schedule private and public launches (as soon as an ISBN and cover image is ready)
Create Media Kit
Create postcards (optional) and e-invites for both launches
Order author and review copies

Four weeks prior:
Send author and review copies
Webpage for book created, also added to Book Titles
Website post about book and launch

Three weeks prior:
Event listing on KAC and Kingstonist (launch notice)

Two weeks prior:
Order launch copies
Create and send first media release
Create Facebook event

One week prior:
Send second media release
Posting info in Facebook event
Posting on Wintergreen Studios website
Adding related images to Pinterest album

ON PUBLICATION DAY:
Send email to Wintergreen Studios Press Advisory Board and author: Marketing report and congrats to Facebook, Twitter and Pinterest posting (Pinterest being cover of the book finally)
Resend emails to all potential reviewers

Day after publication day:
Private launch

Monday after publication day:
Final media release

Thursday after publication day:
Public launch

Other details about book publicity

Media Kit
The media kit is sent to potential reviewers and put on the website page for each book. It should include the following elements:
1. Cover of book
2. Ordering info
3. Contact info
4. Author bio
5. Preview of writing
6. Description of Wintergreen Studios Press
7. Optional: Book list
8. Optional: the workshops and activities out at Wintergreen Studios.

Print Publicity for Books
If the demographic is older, a postcard invitation is recommended in addition to e-invite
Rack Cards or Postcards are recommended for every book, if possible

Private Launch
- ✓ Should take place the Sunday after the Saturday pub date
- ✓ Schedule for posting, Tweeting, etc, should be followed
- ✓ Mainly for authors' friends and family, and for Wintergreen supporters
  E-invite, or in some circumstances a postcard invite, should be created.
- ✓ Private launches will take place at a Kingston location, such as the library, or at Wintergreen, where the venue fee is free or very low.
- ✓ Private launches should come before public launches, as Wintergreen is able to sell books at full price with direct sales.
- ✓ Rena introduces author, author reads, book selling before and after, book signing after
- ✓ Usually an afternoon event 2-4pm in Spring, 1-3pm in Fall

Public Launch
- ✓ Should take place the Thursday following the pub date.
- ✓ Mainly for public announcement of book, and to support local bookstore
- ✓ E-invite only form of direct publicity
- ✓ Mentioned in the Media Kit
- ✓ Schedule for posting, Tweeting, etc, should be followed
- ✓ Evening event: 7-9pm (or 7-8:30pm if at Novel Idea)

Marketing

The Marketing and Communications Director, in collaboration with the Executive Director and Education and Outreach Coordinator, takes charge of all marketing activities.

Regular marketing procedures are in place, and include the following:

- Posters for all workshops and dinner events, designed by the Marketing and Communications Director and distributed to locations in Perth, Westport, and Kingston
- Ongoing electronic posts on the Wintergreen Studios and Wintergreen Studios Press websites as appropriate
- Frequent posts on Facebook and Twitter regarding events, workshops, and retreats
- Print advertising for dinner events and some workshops in *The Frontenac News* and other local newspapers
- Postcards (4x6) with annual listings of workshops and events printed in February of each year
- Trade shows as appropriate
- Annual report printed and made available on the website in September of each year
- Ongoing development of the Wintergreen Studios (www.wintergreenstudios.com) and Wintergreen Studios Press (www.wintergreenstudiospress.com) websites. From time to time this development includes contracting Jon Gustaffson for assistance (jongustaffson@gmail.com).
- Free e-listings in various sites, as appropriate

Finance

Bookkeeping and Records

Revenues and expenses

Revenues are collected by cash, cheque, and Visa. The Executive Director, Operations Manager, and Marketing and Communications Director all have authority to issue invoices (see sample in Appendix) and to collect revenues. Separate numbering streams are used for invoices issued by different members of the Wintergreen staff.

The Executive Director makes deposits on an as-needed basis. Wintergreen's business account is with ScotiaBank at 168 Wellington St., Kingston, ON K7L 3E4 (613 544 3033). The account number is **25296 002 0000310.** All deposits are coded based on the Chart of Accounts provided by the bookkeeper (see Appendix). Deposits are generally made by the Executive Director. However, from time to time, the Operations Manager makes deposits when the Executive Director is unable to do so in a timely manner.

The Executive Director, Operations Manager, and Marketing and Communications Director all have authority to process Visa accounts. Our Visa Merchant number is **873 839 50011.** We use the PayTech system to process Visa transactions by phone (**1 800 503 1035**).

All invoices are submitted to the Executive Director as generated, and the Executive Director provides these invoices to the bookkeeper on a monthly basis. Our bookkeeper is Donna Poirier, DPFS. Her email contact is poirier.donna@gmail.com. When required, receipts are provided upon payment of invoices, although this is not done in all instances. The Executive Director, Operations Manager, and Marketing and Communications Director all have the authority to issue receipts. Each uses her own numbering system.

Expenses are paid directly to suppliers of goods and services by cash, cheque, or credit card. Whenever possible, the Wintergreen American Express card is used for expenses. Both the Executive Director and the Facilities Manager have Wintergreen American Express cards.

If staff or volunteers pay for items directly, they are reimbursed by the Executive Director upon receipt of an invoice and original receipts. Payments are made either by corporate cheque or by electronic transfer.

The Executive Director has signing authority for corporate cheques.

Monthly reports

The Executive Director provides the following to the bookkeeper on a monthly basis:

- ✓ Summary of revenues as indicated by event contracts and invoices
- ✓ Summary of expenses, indicating if the expenses have been paid by WG (cheque or American Express) or by the Executive Director
- ✓ Statements received from Wintergreen
- ✓ Monthly bank statement
- ✓ HST information
- ✓ Updates on accounts receivable
- ✓ Copies of monthly deposit statements coded by the Chart of Accounts

The Bookkeeper provides the following to the Executive Director on a monthly basis, which the Executive Director then forwards to the Secretary-Treasurer and the Board of Directors quarterly, or more frequently if required for crucial financial decisions between Board meetings. Samples of these documents appear in the Appendices.

- ✓ Comparative balance sheet
- ✓ Comparative income statement
- ✓ Budget tracking
- ✓ Aged accounts receivable

HST, Year-end, and employment

The bookkeeper makes quarterly HST reports and payments as required. Our Business/HST number is *No. 834231417 RT0001*. The bookkeeper also prepares the summaries needed for the annual year-end statement, which is prepared by Collins Blay & Co in Kingston, ON. Finally, the bookkeeper manages all of the employment contracts in terms of monthly contributions to CPP, EI, taxes, etc., and the issuance of T4 statements as required.

Grant tracking

The Executive Director works in collaboration with the bookkeeper to track grants in terms of activities and expenditures on an as-needed basis.

Donations

Donations to Wintergreen are receipted by the Secretary-Treasurer. Details are provided regarding the nature of the contribution (e.g., personal or business; cash or in-kind), the contributor, the amount, the date of contribution, and the address of the contributor. The Secretary-Treasurer issues receipts in compliance with Wintergreen's status as a Charitable Organization, including the Charitable Registration Number (*No. RR0001 834231417*) and the CRA website (www.cra.gc.ca/charities)

Online contributions, through the Canada Helps organization, are receipted directly from Canada Helps.

The Executive Director keeps an up-to-date spreadsheet detailing contribution amounts and types for both direct and online contributions.

Appendices
Privacy Statement

In the interest of protecting the rights and privacy of visitors to Wintergreen Studios, the Board of Directors has adopted the following policies.

Wintergreen Studios will not collect any confidential or sensitive information from our visitors (including volunteers, staff, and guests) without their knowledge and consent, and such information will be limited to that which is needed to properly service and support the wishes and requirements of our volunteers, participants, and guests and prospective volunteers, participants, and guests.

The registration form for workshops, meetings, and retreats is the mechanism used to collect information from our guests. If you register for a workshop, meeting, or retreat using our registration form, subscribe for news updates, or otherwise deal directly with Wintergreen Studios, your contact information and a transaction history will be retained by Wintergreen Studios. We will use this information to send you Wintergreen communications, such as emails to inform you of upcoming events.

We do not sell rent, or donate your email addresses and telephone numbers. You can remove yourself from Wintergreen's mailing list at any time by emailing info@wintergreenstudios.com with the term "unsubscribe" in the subject line.

Any information about our guests, staff, or volunteers that is collected will be used only as necessary to service and support guest and participant requests and, unless required by law, will not be released to any third party for any reason.

If you have questions regarding our privacy policy, please contact us by email at info@wintergreenstudios.com or by mail at Wintergreen Studios, PO Box 75, Yarker, ON K0K 3N0

Online Forms for Registration

Workshops

Register Here

Workshops and Retreats

Use this form to register for workshops, meetings, and retreats. A $100 non-refundable deposit is required upon registration, with the balance due when you arrive at Wintergreen. The balance is payable by cheque, cash, or Visa.

You may submit both your registration information and deposit online using a credit card on the PayPal website (PayPal will pop up automatically after you fill out the registration). If you have any questions, please send an e-mail to karen@wintergreenstudios.com. You will be contacted within three business days to complete your registration request.

There is a charge of $25 for NSF cheques. Wintergreen Studios also reserves the right to charge a cancellation fee for registrants who cancel less than 48 hours before a workshop or retreat is scheduled to begin.

Name *

First   Last

Address *

Street Address

Address Line 2

City   State / Province / Region

                Canada

Postal / Zip Code   Country

Email *

EDUCATION & RETREAT CENTRE

Wintergreen Studios is a year-round wilderness education and retreat centre in Southeastern Ontario offering workshops and meeting facilities. Wintergreen enables people to engage in mindful living and return to their homes and workplaces inspired and refreshed.

FOLLOW US

LINKS

- iSCORE News
- Make A Donation
- Ontario Trillium Foundation
- Wintergreen Renewable Energy Co-op
- Wintergreen Studios Press

PAGES

- Reserve Cabins for Private Retreats
- Volunteer Application

THOUGHT TO PONDER

"Men argue; nature acts."

- Voltaire

SHARE ON FACEBOOK

Find us on Facebook

Daytime Phone Number *

___ - ___ - ____
####

Evening Phone Number

___ - ___ - ____
####

Gender *
○ Male ○ Female

Program Information *
○ Fused Glass with Kevin Kapler
○ Songwriting with Ian Tamblyn 2013
○ Lawrence Hill 2013
○ Holly Dean – Must Journals 2013
○ Cordwood Building 2013
○ Helen Humphreys & Kelley Aitken 2013
○ Lorna Crozier 2013

Have you attended a program at Wintergreen already this season? *
○ Yes ● No

Accommodation Options *
○ Facilities and meals only (not staying overnight)
○ Rooms – shared room with twin beds
○ Rooms – private room with double bed
○ Room – private room with double bed (shared)
○ Cabins – Hobbit House, Parthenon, or Meadow Hut
○ Tenting

Dietary Requirements
○ No seafood or shellfish   ○ Vegetarian
○ Sugar free   ○ No spice, onion, or garlic
○ Non-dairy   ○ Gluten free
○ Vegan   ○ No bell peppers

Comments?

How did you hear about Wintergreen Studios?
○ Friend or Colleague   ○ Poster or Flyer
○ Internet Search   ○ Newspaper or Magazine
○ Radio or Television   ○ Other

Please indicate, below, if you would like to be added to our mailing list for information about future events, workshops, and retreats.
○ YES   ○ NO

I agree to pay a non-refundable cancellation fee of $100
*

○ Yes

[Submit]

Cancellations and Transfers

Your deposit is non-refundable. If you cancel your reservation, you can apply the deposit to another program this year or next, or you can transfer the credit to another person. If we cancel a program, you will have the choice of a refund of your deposit or 15% off another program and accommodation package this year or next. If you are flying to Kingston, please check with your airline about its cancellation policy, as Wintergreen is not responsible for travel reservations that have been booked to attend programs that have been cancelled.

Please read our Privacy Statement.

Dinner-Entertainment Evenings

Registration

Purchase Event Tickets and Reserve Accommodations

Use this form to register for dinner-entertainment events. Tickets are $40 each, and include dinner, entertainment, and HST. You may submit both your registration information and ticket fees online using a credit card on the PayPal website (PayPal will pop up automatically after you fill out the registration). Or, if you prefer, you can send a cheque to Wintergreen Studios, PO Box 75, Yarker, ON, K0K 3N0.

If you have any questions, please send an e-mail to karen@wintergreenstudios.com. You will be contacted within three business days.

Name *

First   Last

Email *

Best Phone Number

\#\#\#   \#\#\#   \#\#\#\#

Total $0.00

Select the evening event you want to attend *

○ Ian Tamblyn
○ Triola
○ Lawrence Hill
○ The Gertrudes
○ Swamp Ward Orchestra
○ Lorna Crozier
○ Together in Time
○ Andy Fisher

Number of tickets *

○ 1 ○ 2 ○ 3 ○ 4 ○ 5

Will you be staying overnight? Select the number of guests ($80 extra per person) *

○ No ○ 1 ○ 2 ○ 3 ○ 4 ○ 5

Dietary Requirements

○ No seafood or shellfish   ○ Vegetarian
○ Sugar free   ○ No spice, onion, or garlic
○ Non-dairy   ○ Gluten free
○ Vegan   ○ No bell peppers

Other dietary concerns? Any questions about the event?

Please indicate if you would like to be added to our mailing list for information about future events, workshops, and retreats.

○ YES   ○ NO

[Submit]

Share / Save

Cabin Retreats

Reserve Cabins for Private Retreats

Reserve Cabins for Private Retreats

Use this form to register for private retreats at the Hobbit House, the Beach House, the Parthenon, or the Paddy's Lake Cabin (by special arrangement). After filling out your registration information, you will be prompted to pay for your stay using the PayPal website. Totals include HST. The payment is fully refundable for up to 7 days before your booking. Bookings that are cancelled within the 7 day period are transferable but non-refundable.

We have two rates for cabin rentals. The small wilderness cabins (Parthenon and Hobbit House) are at the basic rate. Premium cabins (Beach House, Paddy's Lake Cabin) are slightly more expensive. If you want a premium cabin, skip over the section which details the wilderness cabins. All of the cabins are exquisitely primitive – no running water, outdoor "facilities," and minimal cooking facilities.

If you have any questions about the cabins or you wish further information about available dates, please send an e-mail to info@wintergreenstudios.com. You will be contacted within three business days.

After we receive your registration and payment, you will be sent an electronic document detailing directions for hiking out to your cabin, directions about how to use the facilities (e.g., the woodstove), what to bring and what to wear, and emergency protocols. Linens are provided.

Enjoy our glorious wilderness!

Name *

[_____] [_____]
First   Last

Total $0.00

Email *

[_____]

Best Phone Number

[____] – [____] – [_____]
 ###   ###   ####

Select the wilderness cabin your wish to rent:

○ Hobbit House
○ Parthenon

What are your preferred dates?

[   ]

I'm coming on my own to one of the wilderness cabins for...

○ One night ($75/night +HST)
○ Two nights ($75/night +HST)
○ Three nights ($75/night +HST)
○ Four nights ($60/night +HST)
○ Five nights ($60/night +HST)
○ Six nights ($60/night +HST)

I will be coming with a companion to a wilderness cabin for...
- ○ One night ($95/night + HST)
- ○ Two nights ($95/night + HST)
- ○ Three nights ($95/night + HST)
- ○ Four nights ($80/night + HST)
- ○ Five nights ($80/night + HST)
- ○ Six nights ($80/night + HST)

Select the premium cabin your wish to rent:
- ○ Beach House (near lodge)
- ○ Paddy's Lake Cabin (please check availability first)

I'm coming on my own to a premium cabin for...
- ○ One night ($95/night +HST)
- ○ Two nights ($95/night +HST)
- ○ Three nights ($95/night +HST)
- ○ Four nights ($80/night +HST)
- ○ Five nights ($80/night +HST)
- ○ Six nights ($80/night +HST)

I will be coming with a companion to a premium cabin for...
- ○ One night ($125/night + HST)
- ○ Two nights ($125/night + HST)
- ○ Three nights ($125/night + HST)
- ○ Four nights ($100/night + HST)
- ○ Five nights ($100/night + HST)
- ○ Six nights ($100/night + HST)

RELEASE OF LIABILITY: In submitting this registration, I agree to obey all posted instructions and observe warnings. I recognize that there are inherent risks associated with wilderness stays, and I assume full responsibility for personal injury to me and/or my companion(s).
- ● Agree
- ○ Do not agree

Emergency Contact *

Please indicate if you would like to be added to our mailing list for information about events, workshops, and retreats.
- ○ YES
- ○ NO

[Submit]

Share / Save

Weddings and Other Special Events

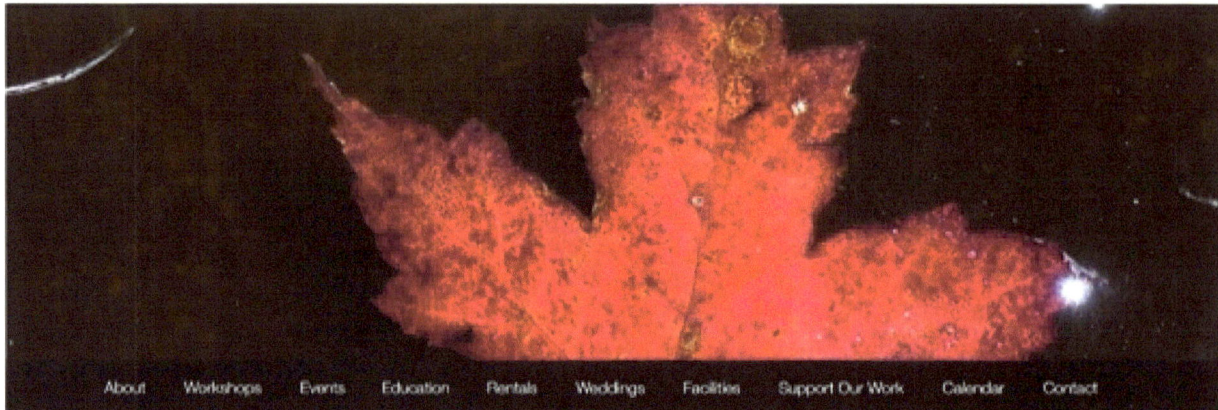

Reserve Accommodations for Special Events

Reserve Accommodations for Special Events

Use this form to register for special events, such as weddings or family retreats. After filling out your registration information, you will be prompted to pay a deposit online using a credit card on the PayPal website (PayPal will pop up automatically after you fill out the registration), with the balance payable by cash, cheque, or Visa upon arrival at Wintergreen.

If you have any questions, please send an e-mail to info@wintergreenstudios.com. You will be contacted within three business days.

Name *

First   Last

Email *

Best Phone Number

####

Select the special event you plan to attend *
- ○ Min-Hi & Ben
- ○ David & Birgit

Total	$50.00
1	$50.00

EDUCATION & RETREAT CENTRE

Wintergreen Studios is a year-round wilderness education and retreat centre in Southeastern Ontario offering workshops and meeting facilities. Wintergreen enables people to engage in mindful living and return to their homes and workplaces inspired and refreshed.

FOLLOW US

LINKS
- iSCORE News
- Make A Donation
- Ontario Trillium Foundation
- Wintergreen Renewable Energy Co-op
- Wintergreen Studios Press

PAGES
- Reserve Cabins for Private Retreats

THOUGHT TO PONDER

"If we change the stories we live by, quite possibly we change our lives."

Dietary Requirements

- ○ No seafood or shellfish
- ○ Vegetarian
- ○ Sugar free
- ○ No spice, onion, or garlic
- ○ Non-dairy
- ○ Gluten free
- ○ Vegan
- ○ No bell peppers

Other dietary concerns? Any questions about the event?

Please indicate if you would like to be added to our mailing list for information about future events, workshops, and retreats.

- ○ YES
- ○ NO

How many people are in your party?

⦿ 1 ○ 2 ○ 3 ○ 4 ○ 5 or more

Which type of accommodation do you prefer?

- ⦿ Single room in the Wintergreen lodge
- ○ Shared accommodations in the Wintergreen lodge
- ○ A cabin in the woods
- ○ Tenting

[Submit]

Share / Save ...

Mailing List

Sample Contract for Workshop Instructor

Memorandum of Agreement
between
Wintergreen Studios, Inc. (hereafter "Wintergreen")
and
Lawrence Hill (hereafter "Instructor")

This agreement details the timelines, expectations, roles, and responsibilities of Wintergreen and the instructor for a Writers' Retreat to be held at Wintergreen Studios, from Friday afternoon April 26th until Sunday afternoon April 28th, 2013. Please sign a copy of the agreement and return the agreement to Wintergreen by surface mail or return an electronic copy to info@wintergreenstudios.com.

WINTERGREEN WILL:

- Provide accommodation for the instructor during the course of the workshop at Wintergreen, as well as for the night before the workshop begins and the night after the workshop ends.
- Pay the instructor a stipend of $2,000.00 + $260.00 HST
- Provide facilities for workshop instruction and meals for the instructors and participants during the course of the workshop

THE RETREAT COORDINATOR WILL:

- Prepare a description of the workshop suitable for publication on the Wintergreen website
- Instruct up to 10 participants and provide follow up as required

_____   April 3, 2013
Rena Upitis, Wintergreen Studios   Date

_____   _____
Lawrence Hill, Instructor   Date

Please note that Wintergreen Studios does not issue T4A slips for tax purposes. It is up to individual instructors to keep records of stipends earned through teaching at Wintergreen Studios. Wintergreen Studios reserves the right to re-negotiate the stipend or to cancel the workshop if fewer than 8 participants register a week before the workshop is scheduled to begin.

Charitable No. 834231417 RR0001 Business No. 834231417 RT0001

WINTERGREEN STUDIOS

Mailing Address: P.O. Box 75 • Yarker ON • K0K 3N0 • (613) 273-8745 • www.wintergreenstudios.com
Location: 9780 Canoe Lake Road, Township of South Frontenac ON

Sample Letter to Workshop Participants

Hello everyone!

The workshop with Lawrence Hill begins 4:00 pm Friday afternoon April 26th, 2013 and ends Sunday evening after dinner. We look forward to welcoming you to Wintergreen. Please feel free to arrive any time after 3 pm on Friday, at which time your rooms will be ready. For those of you arriving from out of town the day before, we will be happy to greet you whenever you make your way to Wintergreen. For those of you who have chosen the off site option, the same timing applies as you will be joining us for all meals (breakfast, lunch and dinner). On Sunday, you can expect to be leaving after dinner or earlier if you need to.

After you get settled, we will have an opportunity to introduce you to the facilities at Wintergreen. Any food restrictions have been noted, so we expect to feed each and every one of you with lovely meals during your stay, taking into account all of your dietary needs. Please feel free to bring your own alcoholic beverages, as we do not have a license to serve you. There will be staff and volunteers ready to assist throughout the weekend, and we hope you will enjoy meeting or re-acquainting yourself the staff on hand for your workshop.

If you haven't already done so, you might like to look at our website (www.wintergreenstudios.com) to learn more about our off-grid facilities. The trails are beautiful for hiking, and although the lake is available for swimming it is a 20-minute walk through the woods, so bring your hiking boots and swim gear if you'd like to enjoy the land during your stay. The website also outlines other items that are wise to bring (and not to bring—like hairdryers!). Please be aware that there are ticks in the woods; it is best to wear long sleeves and pants when journeying to the lake or enjoying our other trails.

Reception for cell phones at Wintergreen is limited. We do have a landline should you need to make a phone call or receive calls. We have relatively-high-speed Internet wireless service, so the use of personal computers for off-line and online work is available. We also have a printer and photocopier for your use.

Directions for reaching Wintergreen appear on our website. The address is 9780 Canoe Lake Rd., South Frontenac. If you are using a GPS or Google Maps to get here, ignore the parts about taking the James Wilson Road or the New Road—those tracks can hardly be called roadways. So in other words, if you can take a moment to print the directions from our website, you will be rewarded with wider roads with better gravel! Please be careful on the Wintergreen laneway as it is a gravel road with uneven ground in spots.

For those of you who owe balances we will accept payment when you arrive. Although we do accept VISA (only VISA), cash or personal cheques are preferred. If you would like to know your balance please email me (wintergreenstudios99@gmail.com) for that information. Please remember that HST will be included in the overall balance.

Warm regards,

Diane Black, Operations Manager

Sample Invoice

Bill To: Invoice #: 1309

Invoice Date: April 13, 2013

Accounts Payable
Centre for the Study of Learning and Performance (CSLP)
Concordia University
Montreal, QC

iSCORE Meeting April 10-12, 2013

Date	Description	
April 10-13	Accommodations and all meals ($130/day)	$390.00
	HST (13%)	$50.70
	Balance due	**$440.70**

Please make cheque payable to:

Wintergreen Studios
PO BOX 75, Yarker, ON K0K 3N0

HST Registration/Business *No. 83423 1417 RT0001*

Sample Receipt for Charitable Donations

WINTERGREEN
STUDIOS
9780 Canoe Lake Road
PO Box 75
Yarker, ON K0K 3N0

www.wintergreenstudios.com
613 • 273 • 8745

OFFICIAL RECEIPT FOR INCOME TAX PURPOSES
Charitable No. 834231417 RR0001 Business No. 834231417 RT0001

In accordance with Canada Revenue Agency *www.cra-arc.gc.ca/charities*

Received March 20, 2013 from:

    NAME
    Address Line 1
    Address Line 2
    Address Line 3

Date: **March 23, 2013**
Amount: **$50.00**
Type: **Personal**
Receipt #: **13036**

_____
Helen Turnbull, Secretary-Treasurer

Receipts are numbered sequentially. The first two numbers indicate the tax year of the donation; the remaining three numbers refer to the numbered receipted donation, with the first receipt each year beginning with 001.

The Secretary-Treasurer signs all receipts except those for donations made by the Secretary-Treasurer and/or the Secretary-Treasurer's family. These donations are signed by the President.

The Secretary-Treasurer mails receipts to donors, often including a personal note regarding the donation.

Chart of Accounts

	No.	Description	Type	
mASSET				
	1000	**Current Assets**	H	
	1050	Petty Cash	A	Inventory
	1055	Cash on hand for deposit	A	Bank
	1060	Chequing Bank Account	A	Bank
	1067	Foreign Currency Bank	A	Bank
	1070	Acct Receivable - NSF ck	A	Asset
	1075	Total Cash	S	
	1083	MasterCard Receivable	G	Credit Card Receivable
	1087	American Express Receivable	G	Credit Card Receivable
	1089	Other Credit Card Receivable	G	Credit Card Receivable
	1100	Investments	G	Marketable Securities
	1200	Accounts Receivable	G	Accounts Receivable
	1201	Accounts Receivable	G	Asset
	1205	Allowance for Doubtful Accounts	G	Allowance for Bad Debts
	1210	Accounts Receivable – GST	G	Asset
	1300	Prepaid Insurance	G	Asset
	1320	Prepaid Expenses	G	Other Current Asset
	1400	**Total Current Assets**	T	
	1700	**Capital Assets**	H	
	1810	Leasehold Improvements	A	Capital Asset
	1815	Accum Amort – Road	A	Asset
	1817	Net - Leasehold Improvements	S	
	1820	Furniture & Equipment	A	Capital Asset
	1825	Accum. Amort. -Furn. & Equip.	A	Accum. Amort. & Depreciation
	1830	Net - Furniture & Equipment	S	
	1840	Vehicle	A	Capital Asset
	1845	Accum. Amort. –Vehicle	A	Accum. Amort. & Depreciation
	1850	Net – Vehicle	S	
	1860	Building	A	Capital Asset
	1865	Accum. Amort. –Building	A	Accum. Amort. & Depreciation
	1870	Net – Building	S	
	1880	Land	G	Capital Asset
	1890	**Total Capital Assets**	T	
	1900	**Other Non-Current Assets**	H	
	1910	Computer Software	G	Other Non-Current Asset
	1930	Incorporation Cost	G	Other Non-Current Asset
	1950	**Total Other Non-Current Assets**	T	

LIABILITY

2000	**Current Liabilities**		H		
2100	Accounts Payable		G	Accounts Payable	
	2101	Accounts Payable - Accountant		G	Liability
	2110	Accrued Liabilities		G	Liability
	2120	Bank Loan		G	Short Term Debt
	2133	Visa Payable		A	Credit Card Payable
	2134	MasterCard Payable		A	Credit Card Payable
	2135	American Express Payable		A	Credit Card Payable
	2140	Other Credit Card Payable		A	Credit Card Payable
	2145	Total Credit Card Payables		S	
	2160	Corporate Taxes payable		G	Income Tax Payable
	2170	Vacation payable		G	Other Payable
	2180	EI Payable		A	Payroll Tax Payable
	2185	CPP Payable		A	Payroll Tax Payable
	2190	Federal Income Tax Payable		A	Payroll Tax Payable
	2195	Total Receiver General		S	
	2220	EHT Payable		G	Payroll Tax Payable
	2230	WSIB Payable		G	Payroll Tax Payable
	2234	User-Defined Expense 1 Payable		G	Payroll Tax Payable
	2235	User-Defined Expense 2 Payable		G	Payroll Tax Payable
	2236	User-Defined Expense 3 Payable		G	Payroll Tax Payable
	2237	User-Defined Expense 4 Payable		G	Payroll Tax Payable
	2238	User-Defined Expense 5 Payable		G	Payroll Tax Payable
	2240	Deduction 1 Payable		G	Employee Deductions Payable
	2250	Deduction 2 Payable		G	Employee Deductions Payable
	2260	Deduction 3 Payable		G	Employee Deductions Payable
	2270	Deduction 4 Payable		G	Employee Deductions Payable
	2280	Deduction 5 Payable		G	Employee Deductions Payable
	2300	PST Payable		G	Sales Tax Payable
	2310	GST/HST Charged on Sales - 13%		A	Sales Tax Payable
	2312	GST Charged on Sales - 5%		A	Sales Tax Payable
	2314	Gst/Hst on Capital - 100% input		A	Liability
	2315	GST/HST(50%) Federal Paid		A	Sales Tax Payable
	2316	GST/HST(82%) Provincial Paid		A	Sales Tax Payable
	2320	GST Payroll Deductions		A	Sales Tax Payable
	2325	GST Adjustments		A	Sales Tax Payable
	2326	Interest on gst assessments		A	Liability
	2327	40% gst collected not remitted		A	Liability
	2328	Force GST		A	Liability
	2330	ITC Adjustments		A	Sales Tax Payable
	2335	GST Owing (Refund)		S	
	2501	Deferred Revenue/Deposits		G	Liability
2599	**Total Current Liabilities**		T		
2600	**Long Term Liabilities**		H		
	2620	Bank Loans		G	Long Term Debt
	2630	Mortgage Payable		G	Long Term Debt
	2680	Loans from Shareholders		G	Long Term Liability
	2690	Loan - Rena Upitis		G	Liability

		2700	Total Long Term Liabilities		T	
EQUITY						
		3300	Share Capital		H	
		3350	Common Shares		G	Share Capital
		3390	Preferred Shares		G	Share Capital
		3400	Total Share Capital		T	
		3500	Retained Earnings		H	
		3560	Retained Earnings - Previous Year		G	Retained Earnings
		3600	Current Earnings	X		Current Earnings
		3690	Total Retained Earnings		T	
REVENUE		4000	Revenue		H	
		4020	Facility Income - Program	G		Operating Revenue
		4024	Facility Income - Rentals	G		Operating Revenue
		4030	Foundations	G		Operating Revenue
		4100	NGO & Partnerships		G	Operating Revenue
		4105	Donations - Non Receipted		G	Operating Revenue
		4110	Donations - Receipted		G	Operating Revenue
		4120	Program Grants - Government		G	Operating Revenue
		4122	Fund Raising		G	Operating Revenue
		4123	Gala		G	Operating Revenue
		4130	Intern Wage Reimbursement		G	Operating Revenue
		4132	Trade Show Revenue		G	Operating Revenue
		4200	Sales		G	Operating Revenue
		4260	Net Sales		T	
		4400	Other Revenue		H	
		4440	Interest Revenue		G	Non-Operating Revenue
		4460	Miscellaneous Revenue		G	Non-Operating Revenue
		4467	Store Sales	G		Revenue
		4468	Shipping		G	Operating Revenue
		4469	Unused		G	Operating Revenue
		4470	Unused		G	Operating Revenue
		4471	Author Order		G	Operating Revenue
		4473	Net Revenue Amazon (online) Sales		G	Operating Revenue
		4480	WSP Direct Sales (100% list)		G	Operating Revenue
		4500	Total Other Revenue		T	
EXPENSE						
		5000	Expenses		H	
		5190	Subcontracts	G		Cost of Goods Sold
		5402	Workshop Food - Program Expense	G		Operating Expense
		5403	Kitchen Supplies & Housekeeping	G		Operating Expense
		5404	Casual Labour - Kitchen		G	Operating Expense
		5408	Honoraria & Stipends		G	Operating Expense

5409	Supplies & Materials		G	Cost of Goods Sold
5410	Salaries - Program & PR Coordinator		G	Payroll Expense
5415	Salaries : Logistics & Operations		G	Operating Expense
5420	EI Expense		G	Payroll Expense
5430	CPP Expense		G	Payroll Expense
5440	WSIB Expense		G	Payroll Expense
5460	EHT Expense		G	Payroll Expense
5464	User-Defined Expense 1 Expense		G	Payroll Expense
5610	Bookkeeping		G	General & Admin. Expense
5612	Professional Fees		G	General & Admin. Expense
5615	Advertising & Promotions		G	General & Admin. Expense
5617	Professional Development		G	Operating Expense
5620	Bad Debts		G	Bad Debt Expense
5625	Consulting Fees		G	General & Admin. Expense
5645	Fundraising		G	Operating Expense
5660	Amortization Expense		G	Amort./Depreciation Expense
5670	Printing		G	Cost of Goods Sold
5671	Shipping		G	Cost of Goods Sold
5685	Insurance		G	General & Admin. Expense
5690	Interest & Bank Charges		G	Interest Expense
5691	Credit Card Discounts		G	Cost of Goods Sold
5692	Interest on Line of Credit		G	Interest Expense
5694	Mortgage Interest		G	Interest Expense
5700	Office Supplies		G	General & Admin. Expense
5702	Postage & Couriers		G	General & Admin. Expense
5704	Web Design/Newsletters		G	Operating Expense
5706	Fuel		G	Operating Expense
5720	Property Taxes		G	General & Admin. Expense
5730	Travel - Program Expense		G	Operating Expense
5731	WSP-Royalties		G	Cost of Goods Sold
5732	WSP-Editing Fees		G	Cost of Goods Sold
5733	WSP-Marketing/Print Materials		G	Cost of Goods Sold
5734	WPS-Launch Expenses		G	Cost of Goods Sold
5735	WSP-Brokerage/Shipping		G	Cost of Goods Sold
5736	WSP-Printing		G	Cost of Goods Sold
5737	WSP-Miscellaneous		G	Cost of Goods Sold
5740	Miscellaneous Expenses		G	General & Admin. Expense
5760	Small tools and repairs		G	General & Admin. Expense
5762	Gardening		G	Cost of Goods Sold
5765	Repair & Maintenance		G	General & Admin. Expense
5770	Memberships & Fees		G	General & Admin. Expense
5780	Telephone & Internet-Mthly-Admin		G	General & Admin. Expense
5784	Hospitality & Travel – Admin		G	General & Admin. Expense
5896	Suspense		G	General & Admin. Expense
5999	**Total General & Admin. Expenses**		T	

Sample Comparative Balance Sheet

ASSET

Current Assets

Chequing Bank Account	978.23		216.99	
Acct Receivable - NSF ck	0.00		0.00	
Total Cash		978.23		216.99
Investments		0.00		-82.95
Accounts Receivable		1,741.48		6,670.50
Due to/from WREC		0.00		0.00
Accounts Receivable - GST		0.00		0.00
Prepaid Insurance		230.67		6,930.83
Prepaid Expenses		632.95		359.41
Total Current Assets		3,583.33		14,094.78

Capital Assets

Leasehold Improvements	16,480.00		16,480.00	
Accum Amort – Road	-3,776.64		-2,472.00	
Net - Leasehold Improvements		12,703.36		14,008.00
Furniture & Equipment	14,137.35		14,137.35	
Accum. Amort. -Furn. & Equip.	-12,550.64		-8,073.67	
Net - Furniture & Equipment		1,586.71		6,063.68
Building	582,195.27		560,137.20	
Accum. Amort. -Building	-102,305.54		-66,277.80	
Net - Building		479,889.73		493,859.40
Total Capital Assets		494,179.80		513,931.08
TOTAL ASSET		497,763.13		528,025.86

LIABILITY

Current Liabilities

Accounts Payable		6,440.30		6,086.87
Accounts Payable - Accountant		1,300.00		0.00
Accrued Liabilities		0.00		0.00
American Express Payable	1,542.65		330.10	
Total Credit Card Payables		1,542.65		330.10
Vacation payable		1,270.59		219.21
EI Payable	-493.67		146.16	
CPP Payable	0.00		242.82	
Federal Income Tax Payable	0.00		24.96	
Total Receiver General		-493.67		413.94

GST/HST Charged on Sales - 13%	308.46	3,746.88
GST Charged on Sales - 5%	22.84	0.00
Gst/Hst on Capital - 100% input	0.00	-0.01
GST/HST(50%) Federal Paid	45.46	-532.52
GST/HST(82%) Provincial Paid	-112.17	669.94
Interest on gst assessments	0.00	0.00
40% gst collected not remitted	0.00	0.00
Force GST	0.00	0.00
GST Owing (Refund)	264.59	3,884.29
Deferred Revenue/Deposits	3,250.00	0.00
Total Current Liabilities	13,574.46	10,934.41
Long Term Liabilities		
Mortgage Payable	250,833.05	274,166.45
Loan - Rena Upitis	20,879.70	11,769.52
Total Long Term Liabilities	271,712.75	285,935.97
TOTAL LIABILITY	285,287.21	296,870.38
EQUITY		
Share Capital		
Common Shares	0.00	0.00
Preferred Shares	0.00	0.00
Total Share Capital	0.00	0.00
Retained Earnings		
Retained Earnings - Previous Year	215,024.86	204,673.62
Current Earnings	-2,548.94	26,481.86
Total Retained Earnings	212,475.92	231,155.48
TOTAL EQUITY	212,475.92	231,155.48
LIABILITIES AND EQUITY	497,763.13	528,025.86

Generated On: 04/05/2013

Sample Comparative Income Statement

	Actual 07/01/2012 to 03/31/2013	Actual 07/01/2011 to 03/31/2012
REVENUE		
Revenue		
Facility Income - Program	35,649.98	24,544.26
Facility Income - Rentals	7,559.82	8,770.75
NGO & Partnerships	0.00	6,760.00
Donations-Non Receipted(Canada Help)	1,201.25	406.20
Donations - Receipted	32,045.00	43,246.48
Program Grants	10,000.00	3,000.00
Fund Raising	0.00	0.00
Gala	0.00	0.00
Intern Wage Reimbursement	0.00	0.00
Trade Show Revenue	0.00	0.00
Sales	0.00	1,396.46
Net Sales	86,456.05	88,124.15
Other Revenue		
Interest Revenue	141.83	-57.53
Miscellaneous Revenue	2,678.78	5,832.12
Store Sales	14,692.65	4,998.00
Shipping	79.87	0.00
unused	0.00	0.00
unused	0.00	0.00
Author Order	23,185.91	0.00
Net Revenue Amazon (online) Sales	1,436.67	0.00
WSP Direct Sales (100% list)	3,179.50	0.00
Total Other Revenue	45,395.21	10,772.59
TOTAL REVENUE	131,851.26	98,896.74
EXPENSE		
Expenses		
Subcontracts	0.00	470.00
Workshop Food - Program Expense	8,161.31	6,092.99
Kitchen Supplies & Housekeeping	1,652.19	432.20
Casual Labour - Kitchen	3,938.34	3,219.60
Honoraria & Stipends	7,897.00	6,950.00
Supplies & Materials	313.34	105.01
Salaries - Program & PR Coordinator	15,279.49	3,266.59
Salaries : Operations Manager	3,634.08	3,693.55
EI Expense	73.12	85.27

CPP Expense	693.90	121.41
Salaries: Marketing/Communications	9,712.50	0.00
Salaries: Kitchen & Housekeeping	3,120.00	0.00
Bookkeeping	1,195.31	1,000.60
Professional Fees	1,463.19	602.10
Advertising & Promotions	684.64	1,683.04
Professional Development	0.00	36.30
Bad Debts	0.00	0.00
Consulting Fees	0.00	0.00
Fundraising	0.00	101.76
Amortization Expense	15,707.65	0.00
Printing	132.32	0.00
Shipping	393.64	0.00
Insurance	8,792.32	1,960.13
Interest & Bank Charges	411.27	512.21
Credit Card Discounts	547.89	0.00
Interest on Line of Credit	0.00	6.50
Mortgage Interest	8,748.78	9,569.13
Office Supplies	109.88	71.37
Postage & Couriers	54.54	315.79
Web Design/Newsletters	133.98	25.47
Fuel	809.27	2,137.13
Property Taxes	9,075.51	11,019.98
Travel - Program Expense	475.77	387.60
WSP-Royalties	1,546.88	0.00
WSP-Editing Fees	0.00	0.00
WSP-Marketing/Print Materials	128.55	0.00
WPS-Launch Expenses	0.00	0.00
WSP-Brokerage/Shipping	9,602.97	11,910.86
WSP-Printing	12,094.06	0.00
WSP-Miscellaneous	25.71	0.00
Miscellaneous Expenses	25.97	0.00
Small tools and repairs	2,355.72	2,145.66
Gardening	1,038.01	43.71
Repair & Maintenance	2,473.81	2,200.54
Memberships & Fees	0.00	406.00
Telephone & Internet-Mthly-Admin	1,433.34	1,340.32
Hospitality & Travel - Admin	463.95	502.06
Total General & Admin. Expenses	134,400.20	72,414.88
TOTAL EXPENSE	134,400.20	72,414.88
NET INCOME	-2,548.94	26,481.86

Sample Aged Accounts Receivable

	Source	Date	Transaction Type	Total	Current	31 to 60	61 to 90	91+
Another Story Bookshop								
	1225	06-29-2012	Invoice	66.15	0.00	0.00	0.00	66.15
Total outstanding:				66.15	0.00	0.00	0.00	66.15
Books on Beechwood								
	1213	05-25-2012	Invoice	66.15	0.00	0.00	0.00	66.15
	1232	07-31-2012	Invoice	110.25	0.00	0.00	0.00	110.25
Total outstanding:				176.40	0.00	0.00	0.00	176.40
indigo Books								
	1306C	04-11-2013	Invoice	141.49	141.49	0.00	0.00	0.00
Total outstanding:				141.49	141.49	0.00	0.00	0.00
iScore Research Project Manager								
	1304	03-18-2013	Invoice	880.18	0.00	880.18	0.00	0.00
	1307	04-11-2013	Invoice	287.10	287.10	0.00	0.00	0.00
	1310	04-13-2013	Invoice	405.80	405.80	0.00	0.00	0.00
	1312	04-17-2013	Invoice	239.85	239.85	0.00	0.00	0.00
Total outstanding:				1,812.93	932.75	880.18	0.00	0.00
U of T Bookstore								
	1301C	01-26-2013	Invoice	110.25	0.00	0.00	0.00	110.25
Total outstanding:				110.25	0.00	0.00	0.00	110.25
Total unpaid invoices:				2,307.22	1,074.24	880.18	0.00	352.80
Total deposits/prepaid order:				0.00	0.00	0.00	0.00	0.00
Total outstanding:				2,307.22	1,074.24	880.18	0.00	352.80

Sample Monthly Budget Report to the Board of Directors

For the period ended	Mar-13	Budget
REVENUE		
Donations (Receipted)	$32,045	**$45,000**
Donations (Unreceipted)	1,201	**500**
NGOs & Partnerships	-	**30,000**
Foundations and Program Grants	10,000	**20,000**
Fundraising		**1,500**
Facility Income: Programs	35,650	**35,000**
Facility Income: Rentals	7,560	**15,000**
Miscellaneous Income (e.g., WSP)	45,395	**45,000**
Total Revenue	**$131,851**	**$192,000**
EXPENSES		
Administrative Expenses		
Office Supplies	110	**250**
Postage & Courier	55	**750**
Bank & Credit Card Fees	548	**750**
Hospitality & Travel	464	**750**
Memberships & Fees	-	**500**
Professional Development	-	**500**
Telecommunications (phone & internet)	1,433	**2,250**
Fundraising	-	**500**
Professional Fees	1,463	**1,500**
Bookkeeping	1,195	**2,000**
Consulting Fees (Evaluation & Reports)	-	**2,000**
Miscellaneous Expenses	26	**1,000**
Total Admin Expenses	**$5,294**	**$12,750**
Program Expenses: Facility & Retreats		
Salaries: Operations Manager	3,634	**6,000**
Salaries: Kitchen & Housekeeping Manager	1,560	**3,500**
Contract Labour (housekeeping, grounds, kitchen)	3,938	**8,000**
Gardening	1,038	**1,500**
Fuel	809	**2,500**
Insurance	8,792	**7,000**
Property Taxes	9,076	**9,000**
Interest on LOC & other banking charges	411	**750**
Interest on Mortgage	8,749	**15,000**
Repairs & Maintenance	4,830	**3,000**
Kitchen & Housekeeping Supplies	1,652	**1,500**
Amortization	15,708	**27,000**
Total Facility Expenses	**$60,197**	**$84,750**

Program Expenses: Workshops & Courses

Salaries: Marketing and Communications	9,713	**20,000**
Salaries: Program & PR Coordinator	16,047	**6,000**
Salaries: Kitchen and Housekeeping Manager	1,560	**3,500**
Food	8,161	**9,000**
Marketing: Advertising & Promotion	685	**1,500**
Wintergreen Studio Press	23,924	**20,000**
Supplies & Materials	313	**500**
Honoraria & Stipends	7,897	**10,000**
Telecommunications (Web design & newsletters)	134	**500**
Travel	476	**2,000**
Total Program Expenses	**$68,909**	**$73,000**
TOTAL EXPENSES	**$134,400**	**$170,500**
NET OPERATING REVENUE	**$(2,549)**	**$21,500**

Volunteer Kit

2016–2018

It is not fair to ask of others what you are not willing to do yourself.

– *Eleanor Roosevelt*

If you want happiness for a lifetime – help the next generation.

– *Chinese Proverb*

If you can't go where people are happier, try to make people happier where you are.

– *Ashleigh Brilliant*

I long to accomplish a great and noble task, but it is my chief duty to accomplish small tasks as if they were great and noble.

– *Helen Keller*

Footprints on the sands of time are not made by sitting down.   – *Proverb*

No one can sincerely try to help another without helping himself.   – *Charles Dudley Warner*

We make a living by what we get, but we make a life by what we give. – *Winston Churchill*

If you want happiness for an hour – take a nap… If you want happiness for a day – go fishing… If you want happiness for a year – inherit a fortune. If you want happiness for a lifetime – help somebody!

– *Unknown*

Life's most persistent and urgent question is: What are you doing for others?

– *Martin Luther King Jr.*

Wintergreen is an educational retreat centre in the Frontenac Arch Biosphere Reserve in Southeastern Ontario. Our work involves three broad foci: education, culture, and the environment. We offer a variety of short courses in the arts, as well as retreat and meeting facilities for individuals and groups. We rent our woodland cabins to people interested in a wilderness retreats. Wintergreen also hosts weddings.

Guests at Wintergreen have access to a network of over a dozen trails for self-guided hikes through the 204-acre property. The land features mixed forests and meadows, granite outcroppings, ponds, marshes, and a glacier carved lake. It is home to a wide range of plant life and wildlife. Our simple and comfortable accommodations include private rooms, shared rooms, woodland cabins, and tenting for those who prefer to sleep under the stars. We serve bountiful meals, featuring local and organic foods, much of which is grown in our own gardens. There are vegetarian and gluten-free options, and we also serve fish, poultry, pork, goat, and beef.

Wintergreen Studios is a not-for-profit organization. We were incorporated in September 2007 and received charitable status in July 2008. The lodge was built in the summer and fall of 2008 and our first workshops were offered in the fall of 2008. In addition to our workshops and retreats, Wintergreen partners with the Wintergreen Renewable Energy Co-operative and is home to Wintergreen Studios Press.

Volunteers at Wintergreen

A willing helper does not wait until he is asked.

Like any other not-for-profit educational centre, Wintergreen thrives on the generosity and goodwill of its friends, members, and participants. We invite contributions of materials, volunteer time, and direct donations to support our work. In addition to volunteering, you can also help by spreading the word about our programs, place, and people.

At the heart of any charitable organization is the cadre of volunteers that keep the organization energized and viable. Wintergreen is no exception. We were overwhelmed by the number of volunteers who helped in the building of our straw bale lodge in 2008. Since then, we have enjoyed the *pro bono* services of volunteers and firms in the following ways:

- Kitchen staff with experience working in community and commercial kitchens volunteering to cook and serve at workshops.
- Graphics design by a student intern who contributed many hours of personal time continuing to refine our materials once the internship had ended.
- Off-grid system maintenance by both student interns and employees who installed our solar-based renewable energy system.
- Media releases through the Frontenac Community Futures Development Corporation.
- Marketing strategy consulting and legal advice from a number of highly successful owners of small businesses and consulting firms.
- Garden planning and planting by a horticulturalist completing an internship at Wintergreen and volunteer gardeners who have continued to support and develop the gardens.
- The design of interactive trails, featuring botany and art-making, by a student intern.

From time to time, we have an opening on the Board of Directors, and Board members are volunteers. They are however, a special type of volunteer. The Board assumes both legal and fiduciary responsibilities for Wintergreen Studios and performs the role of trustees. It is the board that establishes the mission, values and governing policies for Wintergreen. If you are interested in serving on our Board, please contact us directly (info@wintergreenstudios.com).

Potential board members should:

- Be committed to the development of a sustainable society and have an affinity for the arts in all forms—the fine arts, the performing arts, the outdoor arts, and the domestic arts.
- Subscribe to the Mission Statement of Wintergreen Studios.
- Commit to a minimum of three years on the Board, and prepare for and attend all of its meetings (estimated at 3 hours every four months).
- Spend about 2 hours each month in additional Committee or Working Group.
- Meet specific skill and experience gaps as identified by the Board.
- Not represent any other organization or interest that could create a conflict of interest.
- Participate in an introductory period that includes: an exploratory interview with the Chair or designated Board member, an orientation tour of Wintergreen Studios and grounds, and participation in at least one Wintergreen program (if not involved in one previously).

> *It is high time that the ideal of success should be replaced with the ideal of service.*
>
> *– Albert Einstein*

What is in this Volunteer Kit?

This Volunteer Kit has been designed to establish consistency for all Wintergreen volunteers. In this kit, we clarify our values and our philosophy, and communicate our mutual responsibilities and expectations. We have included details about the types of volunteer opportunities and how they relate to our philosophy and our programs. We hope this kit will help you make the most of your volunteer experience with us. We encourage you to review the contents at your leisure to help you become acquainted with Wintergreen. Any comments you may have on how to improve the kit can be passed along to the Volunteer Coordinator, her/his delegate, or the Executive Director.

What kinds of volunteer opportunities can I expect?

Volunteers are an important and integral component of our programs and we are always ready to welcome new members to our team. Every volunteer takes an active role in helping Wintergreen carry out its mission

to provide programs and activities that support education, culture, and the environment. Volunteers are carefully recruited, selected, trained, and supervised to work in partnership with staff. Together we provide programs for adults and youth to promote education and quality of life.

Each volunteer offers a different set of skills and receives different rewards. This information package will help give you a better sense of Wintergreen and the various roles volunteers can play. At the end of the kit, you will find a **Volunteer Application Form**. Once you have read through this information and have decided that you'd like to volunteer with us, please complete the application form and return it to our Volunteer Coordinator. Or, you can fill it out online and it will be automatically sent to our Volunteer Coordinator. We look forward to hearing from you and learning more about your interests in Wintergreen.

Wintergreen has eight 'categories' of volunteers. These categories of interest include:

- program and curriculum development
- kitchen and housekeeping
- Board related activities
- gardens and grounds
- music and art
- design and marketing
- building and carpentry
- administration

Program and Curriculum Development

Program and curriculum development volunteers help develop and deliver workshops and tours offered by Wintergreen, both at the Canoe Lake Road location and in local community venues. Program volunteers are often students in post-secondary programs or retired teachers who wish to apply their years of experience to teaching in another context. We have tours and workshops for youth and adults, many of which occur at Wintergreen itself. Some workshops take place in Perth, Westport, and Kingston, at community centres, schools, and post-secondary settings.

Workshop themes include sustainable building techniques, wind power, solar energy, growing food locally, and reducing consumption. Volunteers who deliver these workshops are provided with presentation materials and receive an orientation session to prepare them to lead workshops successfully.

Kitchen and Housekeeping

Kitchen and housekeeping volunteers help prepare meals and ensure that the facilities are ready for groups using Wintergreen for meetings, workshops, and retreats. Kitchen volunteers can expect to do any number of tasks—gathering produce and herbs from the gardens, preparing fresh fruit and vegetables for meals, taking charge of part of a meal, washing dishes, setting tables—pretty much anything that happens in the

kitchen while preparing and serving a meal to a group ranging from 8 to 80 in size! One of our kitchen volunteers ended up leading the dinner-concert meals for well over a year, and wrote a cookbook before the year was out, called A Taste of Wintergreen.

Housekeeping chores include helping with laundry, preparing guest rooms with fresh linens, bringing flowers from the gardens to decorate rooms, and cleaning, dusting, and sweeping. Our most skilled volunteers in housekeeping have a way of noticing just when the bathrooms have run out of paper towels or when a log of wood needs to be added to the woodstove.

Board

Volunteers with the Wintergreen Studio Board of Directors brainstorm with Board members on the vision and future directions of Wintergreen, develop and analyze policies and strategies along with the Board of Directors, and assist in fundraising and grant writing. For example, one of our Board volunteers has secured funding from several partnering organizations. Another Board volunteer, who works in the field of small business consultation, offered *pro bono* advice to the Wintergreen Board in its second year of operation.

As noted previously, the Board of Directors is, itself, a volunteer board. A considerable level of commitment is required to serve as a Board member. Four of the five Founding Directors remain active as Board members, so we do not often have spots to fill on the Board. But from time to time, we do have an opening on the Board. Please contact the Executive Director directly at rena.upitis@gmail.com if you have an interest in serving on the Board.

Gardens and Grounds

Gardens and grounds volunteers plan, plant, and harvest food from our vegetable and herb gardens, assist with the perennial gardens, and help maintain our network of trails. In other words, our gardens and grounds volunteers dig, rake, hoe, weed, cut, chop, and plant!

A series of perennial gardens surround the Wintergreen lodge. To the west side of the lodge there are vegetable and herb gardens, all of which require maintenance and loving attention. The network of trails—over a dozen in total—criss-cross through 200 acres of woodlands and ponds. The trail maintenance involves trimming trees that have grown over the trails, removing deadwood, and generally sprucing up the walkways. Our maintenance schedule ensures that each trail is trimmed at least once every three years, with the Main Trail to Paddy's Lake receiving maintenance annually.

There are also buildings to maintain at Wintergreen. Besides the main lodge, we have many outbuildings. Some are close to the lodge, and include the outdoor kitchen, root cellar, outhouse, smoke house, the sauna, generator shed, and bake oven. Two other buildings close to the lodge offer guest accommodations, the Beach House and the Meadow Hut. All of these buildings need care and the occasional repair. In the woods, there are an additional three cabins—the Hobbit House, the Parthenon, and Paddy's Lake Cabin. And a few more sheds and outhouses, too! Volunteers who care for our buildings do a number of things, such as cleaning, painting, and small repairs.

Many of our buildings (seven, but who's counting?) are heated with wood. Grounds volunteers often give us a day or two in the summer of wood-cutting and gathering, days for which we are all grateful for in the dead of winter. Some of our deadwood needs to be cut with a chainsaw, so if you have training in the safe operation of chainsaws, we have plenty of wood for you to cut!

Music and Art
Musicians, writers, poets, and artists often donate their time to Wintergreen by offering entertainment at dinner-concerts and/or providing art work for the facilities or for fund-raising events.

Much of the art work displayed in the lodge and in the various outbuildings is original. While some of it was purchased, many of the pieces were donated to Wintergreen by donors and workshop participants. Other donated pieces include some of the pottery and fused glass we use for serving dishes.

From time to time we have a grand event—a gala—and often musicians will volunteer to play at these events to help support Wintergreen.

Design and Marketing
Design and marketing volunteers help create the materials and strategies to promote Wintergreen's activities and messages, including those of the Wintergreen Renewable Energy Co-operative and Wintergreen Studios Press. Design is for both print-based materials as well as electronic materials used on our website and through social media outlets.

Other design work involves creating attractive and informative educational materials. Since one of our areas of work is in education, we are always producing new workshops on various topics related to the arts and environment. Current topics include renewable energy (solar and wind), local food, and traditional building practices.

Building and Carpentry

Builders and carpenters volunteer their services to maintain Wintergreen and its outbuildings, and help deliver workshops on sustainable building practices.

One of the regular workshops at Wintergreen involves building with cord-wood and/or straw bales. Volunteers are always welcome at these workshops—and volunteers at all levels of skill and experience (including complete novices!) are appreciated.

Administration

Administrative volunteers assist office staff with reception, mailings and computer tasks. We are especially grateful to administrative volunteers when it is time for the Annual Giving Campaign (every October) or when we are launching a large gala-type event. The next gala is planned for 2014.

Another type of task that falls under administration is placing posters in strategic locations for workshops and events. Let us know if you'd be willing to do this, and we'll provide a list of venues in your area.

What kind of time commitment is expected from volunteers?

In order to ensure consistency in our programs and services, we ask volunteers to consider committing for one year. We do understand, however, that your schedule might be difficult to predict right now and we're hopeful that you'll stay as long as you can. The amount of time that you volunteer depends on your position. For instance, some of our programs run weekly, some monthly and others are annual or as needed (special events or workshops). Some volunteers work only in the summer months (e.g., those who help out with the gardens and grounds). Board members commit to a minimum 3-year term.

Volunteer placement procedures

All volunteers will complete a Volunteer Application Form and review the policies and procedures for information applicable to volunteers, including the Privacy Statement found in this kit.

Prospective volunteers are interviewed to determine the best possible placement within Wintergreen. Placement depends on the skills, talents and interests of prospective volunteers, as well as opportunities available at the time of the interview. No volunteer will be placed in a position for which she/he is not comfortable. Volunteers will be able to decline a suggested assignment or request a change at any point during their involvement with Wintergreen.

All volunteers under the age of 18 will be given assignments where an adult supports them. All personal information obtained during the provision of volunteer service will be treated as confidential.

Volunteer rights and responsibilities

Orientation and feedback

All volunteers will receive a job description and an orientation/tour of the Wintergreen Studios. Orientation sessions are offered semi-annually, usually in June and September, and on an as-needed basis. Some positions may require specific training in advance, such as the delivery of workshops and tours, but no matter what, while 'on-the-job' you will receive ongoing training and support from staff. It is part of their job to ensure you have all the information you need. All volunteers are encouraged to share experiences, get information and keep in touch with other volunteers and staff. Volunteers are always asked for suggestions. We need to know what you want to know and what you have learned while volunteering for Wintergreen.

Reporting of volunteer hours

All volunteers are asked to report the hours they volunteer. This enables Wintergreen to recognize you for your contribution. Additionally, the number of hours contributed to Wintergreen is often reported when we request grant monies to support our work. Please complete your hours on the available timesheets on a daily basis or simply send an email detailing your hours to the Volunteer Coordinator. The timesheets will be collected by the Volunteer Coordinator, totaled and delivered to the Executive Director.

If you are scheduled for an assignment and you are ill or otherwise absent, please make every effort to find a replacement and advise the program coordinator or team leader.

As a volunteer, you have the right to[2]

- Receive accurate information about Wintergreen Studios and its affiliates
- Receive a clear, comprehensive job description
- Be interviewed and appropriately assigned
- Receive training as required
- Do meaningful and satisfying work
- Be seen as belonging, through inclusion at meetings, social functions, etc.
- Be supported in your role

---

[2] Adapted from "Volunteer Rights and Responsibilities" from the PAVE Volunteer Management Training Kit, and "Sample Volunteer Rights and Responsibilities" from the University of North Carolina, Chapel Hill Department of Recreation and Leisure Studies.

- Be safe on the job
- Have choices and feel comfortable about saying no
- Be consulted on matters that directly or indirectly affect you and your work
- Receive feedback on your work
- Receive recognition for your contributions
- Have your personal information be kept confidential
- Be trusted with confidential information if it is necessary in order to do your job

As a volunteer, you are expected to

- Be reliable and punctual, and let your supervisor know if your plans change
- Record all hours of service
- Be trustworthy
- Respect confidentiality
- Respect the rights of people you work with
- Have a non-judgmental approach
- Carry out the specified job description
- Give feedback (e.g., participate in evaluations when asked)
- Be accountable and accept feedback
- Be committed to our vision and program
- Avoid overextending yourself
- Acknowledge decisions made by Wintergreen staff
- Address areas of conflict with the appropriate staff member or Volunteer Coordinator
- Undertake training
- Ask for support when it is needed
- Stay safe on the job
- Bring the priceless gifts of enthusiasm, ideas and energy to your time at Wintergreen!

How are volunteers recognized?

We recognize our volunteers in many ways, both formally and informally. For example, volunteers often go home laden with delicious leftover food, and enjoy free entertainment and reduced prices for workshops. We recognize volunteers by name during events and in our print documents, including the Annual Report which is available in print form and on our website. Above all, we show them respect. And working at Wintergreen is *fun*.

Another formal and visible way of recognizing volunteers is through our annual appreciation lunch. This is held each fall, and is a celebratory gathering of volunteers, donors, and other friends of Wintergreen.

OK—I'd like to volunteer. What do I do next?

Follow these three steps!

Step #1: Send us your completed Volunteer Application Form. There are three easy ways:

Fill out the online form at http://www.wintergreenstudios.com/support-our-work/

Fill out the paper form and send it by mail: PO Box 75, Yarker, ON K0K 3N0

Fill out the paper form, scan it, and send it by email: info@wintergreenstudios.com

Step #2: Meet the Coordinator of our Volunteer Program for an informal interview. This is a great chance for us to meet each other and make sure that our volunteer opportunities match your goals and expectations.

Step #3: Finalize the details

If you join as a volunteer, we will provide you with all tools you'll need to get started. Wintergreen Studios is a charitable organization (*No. 834231417 RR00001*). Donations are tax deductible.

How to find us

Location: 9780 Canoe Lake Rd., Township of South Frontenac

Mailing address: PO Box 75, Yarker, ON K0K 3N0

Telephone: 613 273 8745

Website: www.wintergreenstudios.com

e-mail: info@wintergreenstudios.com

Directions

Our wilderness retreat centre is located at 9780 Canoe Lake Road, in the Township of South Frontenac, in Southeastern Ontario, fifty minutes north of Kingston. You will need to drive to Wintergreen. We suggest that you use the directions provided below rather than relying on your GPS – or at least, if you're using the GPS or Google Maps, don't go down New Road (a one-lane gravel menace!) or the James Wilson Road (really, these aren't "roads"!).

Approximate driving times to Wintergreen from:

- Kingston: 50 minutes
- Toronto: 3.5 hours
- Ottawa: 2 hoursFrom the EAST (e.g., Kingston):

- Travel WEST on HWY 401.
- Take EXIT 611 and turn NORTH onto PROVINCIAL ROUTE 38 / CR-38 (26 km or 15.5 miles)
- Turn RIGHT (EAST) onto DESERT LAKE ROAD, just past Verona (12 km or 7.5 miles)
- Turn LEFT (NORTH) onto CANOE LAKE ROAD and drive down a narrow gravel road to 9780 (11 km or 6.8 miles)

From the WEST (e.g., Toronto):

- Travel EAST on HWY 401.
- Take EXIT 611 and turn NORTH onto PROVINCIAL ROUTE 38 / CR-38 (26 km or 15.5 miles)
- Turn RIGHT (EAST) onto DESERT LAKE ROAD, just past Verona (12 km or 7.5 miles)
- Turn LEFT (NORTH) onto CANOE LAKE RD and drive down a narrow gravel road to 9780 (11 km or 6.8 miles)

From the NORTH (e.g., Ottawa through Westport):

- Travel WEST on ROUTE 417 W / TRANS CANADA HWY W. to the HWY-7 exit- EXIT 145- toward TORONTO / CARLETON PLACE.
- Merge onto PROVINCIAL ROUTE 7 / TRANS CANADA HWY. (54 km or 33.6 miles)
- Turn LEFT onto WILSON ST W / PROVINCIAL ROUTE 43 / CR-43. (1.3 km or 0.8 miles)
- Turn LEFT onto FOSTER ST / PROVINCIAL ROUTE 43 / CR-43. (<0.16 km or 0.1 miles)
- Turn RIGHT onto GORE ST E / PROVINCIAL ROUTE 43 / CR-43. Continue to follow GORE ST E. (1.3 km or 0.8 miles)
- Turn RIGHT onto SCOTCH LINE RD / CR-10. Continue to follow CR-10 to Westport. (28.6 km or 17.9 miles)
- Turn RIGHT onto BEDFORD ST / CR-12 in downtown Westport. Continue to follow CR-12. (5.6 km or 3.5 miles)
- CR-12 becomes WESTPORT RD/CR-8 (and Salem Rd. in places as well!). (6 km or 3.8 miles)
- Turn LEFT onto CANOE LAKE RD and drive down a narrow gravel road to 9780 (6 km or 3.8 miles)

From the SOUTH (e.g., Syracuse):

- Take I-81 N to cross into Canada
- I-81 N becomes PROVINCIAL ROUTE 137 N (Portions toll over bridges (3.8 km or 2.4 miles)
- Take the HWY-401 W ramp toward KINGSTON / TORONTO. (1.4 km or 0.9 miles)
- Merge onto PROVINCIAL ROUTE 401 W. (49 km or 30.6 miles)
- Take EXIT 611 and turn NORTH onto PROVINCIAL ROUTE 38 / CR-38 (26 km or 15.5 miles)
- Turn RIGHT (EAST) onto DESERT LAKE ROAD, just past Verona (12 km or 7.5 miles)
- Turn LEFT (NORTH) onto CANOE LAKE ROAD and drive down a narrow gravel road to 9780 (11 km or 6.8 miles)

> *Just as there are no little people or unimportant lives, there is no insignificant work.*
>
> *– Elena*

Why volunteer?

People have been offering their skills and spirit to organizations like ours ever since charitable organizations were first developed. Sometimes the time commitment and level of generosity is almost beyond comprehension. Why is that? Perhaps it is because, by volunteering, the volunteer receives just as much—or more—than he or she gives to the organization. Volunteering is about taking action, about having an opportunity to give to others, about joining others in community, about happiness, about leadership, about leading meaningful and fulfilled lives. Read these words and be inspired.

Blessed is the person who sees the need, recognizes the responsibility, and actively becomes the answer.

– William Arthur Ward

Some men see things as they are and say 'why'? I dream things that never were, and say, 'why not'?

– George Bernard Shaw

Great beauty, great strength, and great riches are really and truly of no great use; a great heart exceeds all. *– Benjamin Franklin*

Sometimes our light goes out but is blown into flame by another human being. Each of us owes deepest thanks to those who have rekindled this life. *– Albert Schweitzer*

Blessed is the leader who has sought the high places, but who has been drafted into service because of his ability and willingness to serve.

– Unknown

To give life meaning, one must have a purpose larger than self.

– William Durant

My life belongs to the whole community, and as long as I live it is my privilege to do for it whatever I can. *– George Bernard Shaw*

Half our life is spent trying to find something to do with the time we have rushed through life trying to save. *– Will Rogers*

Only those who attempt the absurd will achieve the impossible.

– Albert Einstein

I don't know what your destiny will be, but one thing I know; the only ones among you who will be really happy are those who have sought and found how to serve.

– Albert Schweitzer

It's no use saying, "We are doing our best." You have got to succeed in doing what is necessary.
–Winston Churchill

Privacy Statement

In the interest of protecting the rights and privacy of visitors to Wintergreen Studios, the Board of Directors has adopted the following policies.

Wintergreen Studios will not collect any confidential or sensitive information from our visitors (including volunteers, staff, and guests) without their knowledge and consent, and such information will be limited to that which is needed to properly service and support the wishes and requirements of our volunteers, participants, and guests and prospective volunteers, participants, and guests.

The registration form for workshops, meetings, and retreats is the mechanism used to collect information from our guests. If you register for a workshop, meeting, or retreat using our registration form, subscribe for news updates, or otherwise deal directly with Wintergreen Studios, your contact information and a transaction history will be retained by Wintergreen Studios. We will use this information to send you Wintergreen communications, such as emails to inform you of upcoming events.

We do not sell rent, or donate your email addresses and telephone numbers. You can remove yourself from Wintergreen's mailing list at any time by emailing info@wintergreenstudios.com with the term "unsubscribe" in the subject line.

Any information about our guests, staff, and volunteers that is collected will be used only as necessary to service and support guest and participant requests and, unless required by law, will not be released to any third party for any reason.

If you have questions regarding our privacy policy, please contact us at info@wintergreenstudios.com or by mail at Wintergreen Studios, PO Box 75, Yarker, ON K0K 3N0

Date Received: _____

Wintergreen Studios Volunteer Application Form

Thank you for your interest in volunteering at Wintergreen Studios. Wintergreen is a community-centered not-for-profit educational retreat centre, where members, volunteers, and staff work together to nourish appreciation for the arts and the natural world. This is achieved through an integrated series of programs, events, and resources offered at or in affiliation with Wintergreen.

First Name: _____ Last Name: _____

Phone: _____

Address: _____

_____

Best time to contact you by phone: _____

Email: _____

How did you learn about volunteering at Wintergreen?

☐ Wintergreen staff/volunteer ☐ Website
☐ Attending an event at Wintergreen ☐ Other _____

What season(s) are you able to volunteer?

☐ Summer ☐ Fall ☐ Winter ☐ Spring

What days of the week work best for you?

- ☐ Monday
- ☐ Tuesday
- ☐ Wednesday
- ☐ Thursday
- ☐ Friday
- ☐ Saturday
- ☐ Sunday

What is your employment status?

- ☐ Employed full-time
- ☐ At-home parent
- ☐ Other_____
- ☐ Student full-time
- ☐ Employed part-time
- ☐ Retired
- ☐ Student part-time

Which areas/programs interest you most (check as many as apply)?

- ☐ Program & curriculum
- ☐ Kitchen & housekeeping
- ☐ Board related activities
- ☐ Gardens and grounds
- ☐ Music and art
- ☐ Design and marketing
- ☐ Building and carpentry
- ☐ Administration
- ☐ Other: _____

What other volunteering have you been involved with?

_____

_____

_____

What are some of your reasons for volunteering? What do you hope to get out of this experience?

_____

_____

_____

Who can we contact as references?

	Name	Phone Number(s)	Relationship
1.	_____	_____	_____
2.	_____	_____	_____
3.	_____	_____	_____

Volunteer statement and signature

I understand that Wintergreen Studios will be collecting, creating, using and disclosing my personal information for the purpose of establishing and managing a volunteer relationship. I consent to Wintergreen doing so, and I also consent to the collection and use of my personal information in order to ensure the safety of Wintergreen participants, for statistical purposes, and to inform me about Wintergreen's programs or services. I consent to the release of my name to Wintergreen's Marketing and Communications Department to further Wintergreen's fundraising activities.

_____   _____

Applicant's Signature   Date

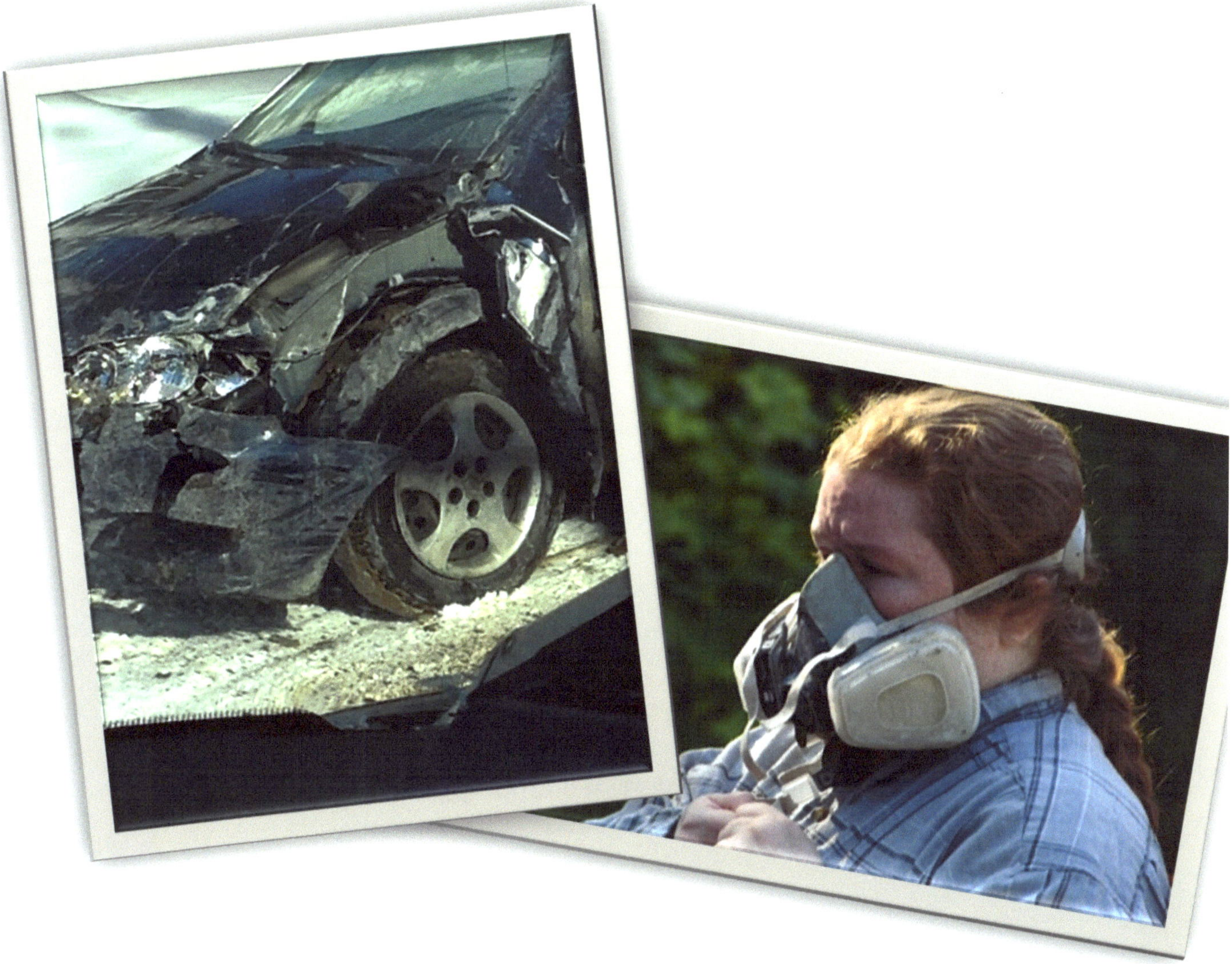

Emergency Handbook

2016–2018

If you can't go where people are happier, try to make people happier where you are.
— *Ashleigh Brilliant*

Ideas without action are useless.
— *Harvey Mackay*

I long to accomplish a great and noble task, but it is my chief duty to accomplish small tasks as if they were great and noble.
— *Helen Keller*

Emergency Handbook

Contact Numbers

AMBULANCE–FIRE–POLICE

911

FIRE:

Local Fire Department: 613 376 3027

POLICE:

OPP Non-emergency dispatch: 1 888 310 1122

Frontenac OPP Detachment (Verona) 613 372 1932

HOSPITALS & MEDICAL CENTRES:

Perth Hospital: 613 267 1500

Kingston General Hospital: 613 548 3232

Hotel Dieu Hospital (Kingston): 613 544 3310

Verona Medical Centre: 613 374 2077

Nearest medical doctor: Dr. Rob Roberts, Westport 613 273 8181

Additional Contacts for Emergencies

Neighbours: David Hahn, Forest Farms 613 273 5545
 Adam Turcotte & Louise Cooper 613 273 9876

Executive Director: Rena Upitis 613 533 6212 (W)
 613 377 6687 (H)

Solar: *Contact for problems with solar panels, batteries, generator back-up, solar hot water heater. Company is Quantum Renewable Energy.*

 Eric Collins 613 217 0690
 Rick Rooney 613 546 2326

KFLA Health: Joanne McGurn 613 279 2151 (W)
 613 634 1908 (H)

Fire Protocol

Fire in Lodge

- Visible signs of fire and/or continuous ringing of a smoke detector unless previously identified as a test
- Any staff member or volunteer, upon finding a fire, shall immediately use fire extinguisher to extinguish small fires in the lodge
- Evacuate the area if fire cannot be extinguished with fire extinguisher
-

Fire in Outbuildings

- Any staff member, guest, or volunteer, upon finding a fire, shall immediately use fire extinguisher to extinguish small fires
- Evacuate the area if fire cannot be extinguished with fire extinguisher and call 911

Pre-Planning

- Ensure guests are aware of exit doors (4 in the lodge)
- Establish clearly defined roles to ensure lodge is empty
- Coordinate modified evacuation for participants or instructors requiring this service
- Post emergency fire numbers in office
- Discuss protocol with instructors and participants
- Establish rendezvous site as the South Meadow

On Hearing the Alarm

Lodge staff will:
- Call 911
- Monitor the exit of participants and instructors to the rendezvous site (South Meadow)
- Sweep main lodge
- Report to other lodge staff in the South Meadow; give/receive reports and coordinate appropriate course of action
- Ensure that all participants and instructors are accounted for
- Take emergency kit to South Meadow

Guests will:
- Exit quickly and remain in the South Meadow until further notice

Injury Protocol

> Examples
>
> MINOR: cuts, scrapes, mild allergic reactions
>
> MAJOR: fractures, serious cuts, collapse, suspected head or back injuries, anaphylactic allergic reactions

Pre-Planning

- Provide staff with first aid training opportunities
- Ensure first aid kits are well stocked
- Ensure first aid kits are clearly organized and accessible
- Follow St. John's Ambulance Training first aid protocols (manual is in the office with first aid kit)

In Case of Serious Injury

- Gather information and keep patient warm and comfortable
- Do not move patient if injury is serious
- Call 911 for an ambulance
- Await further instruction from medical authorities
- Complete and file an incident report form (reports are kept in the office with the first aid kit)

Incident Reports

> Examples
>
> Major injury, Break-in or other criminal offence, Property damage

The incident report forms appear on the following two pages. Extra copies are clipped inside the door of the office at the lodge. Incident report forms for injuries or property damage are printed on yellow paper; incident report forms requiring a police report are printed on green paper.

Wintergreen Studios

Incident Report Form for Personal Injury or Property Damage

Information on injured person or owner of damaged property:

Name: _____

Birthdate: _____

Address: _____

Email: _____

Phone number(s): _____ _____

Information on incident:

Date of incident: _____

Place and nature of activity:

Description of incident and nature of injury or property damage:

Complete if applicable:

Name of doctor or health care practitioner consulted:

_____

Phone: _____ Name of hospital or clinic:

_____

Witness Name: _____ Phone: _____

Witness Name: _____ Phone: _____

Complete only if this incident was reported to police:

Police Station: _____

Police Officer: _____   Phone: _____

Vehicle information if applicable:

Name of owner: _____

Address: _____

Phone number(s): _____   _____

Name of driver: _____

Insurer & Policy #: _____

Reporting person's contact information:

Name: _____

Position at Wintergreen: _____

Address: _____

Email: _____

Phone number(s): _____   _____

Signature and date:

This report must be signed by a Director, the Executive Director, or the Operations Manager of Wintergreen Studios

Name: _____   Date: _____

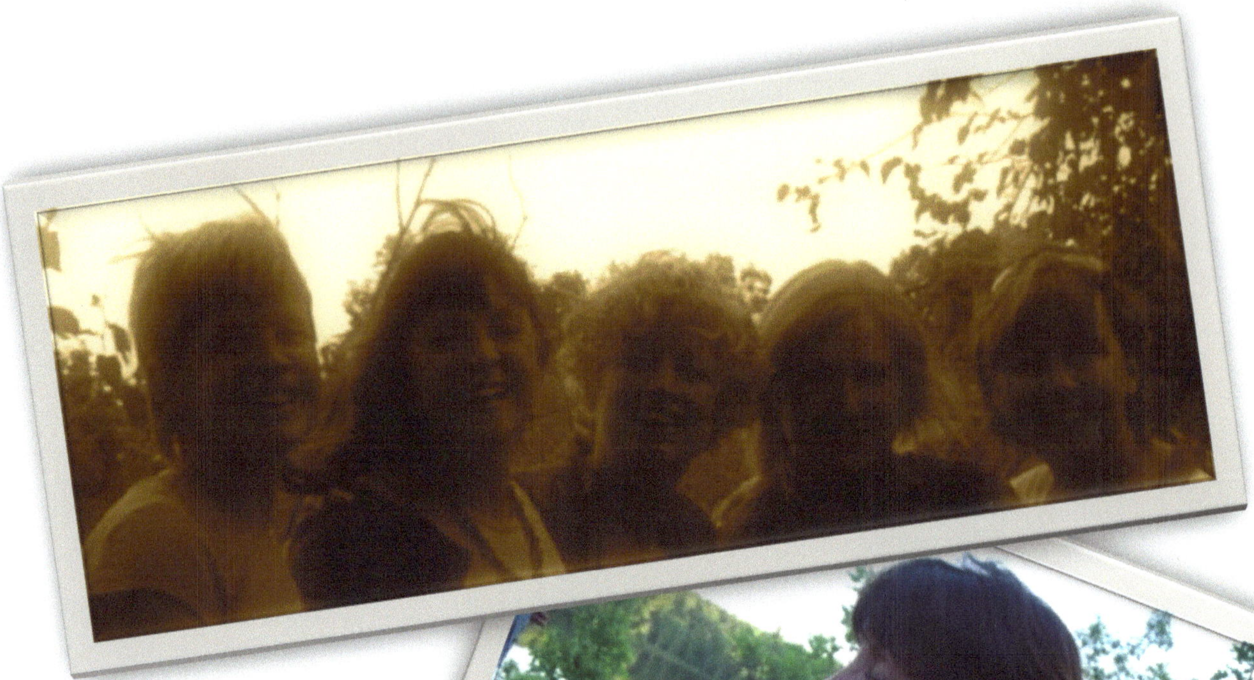

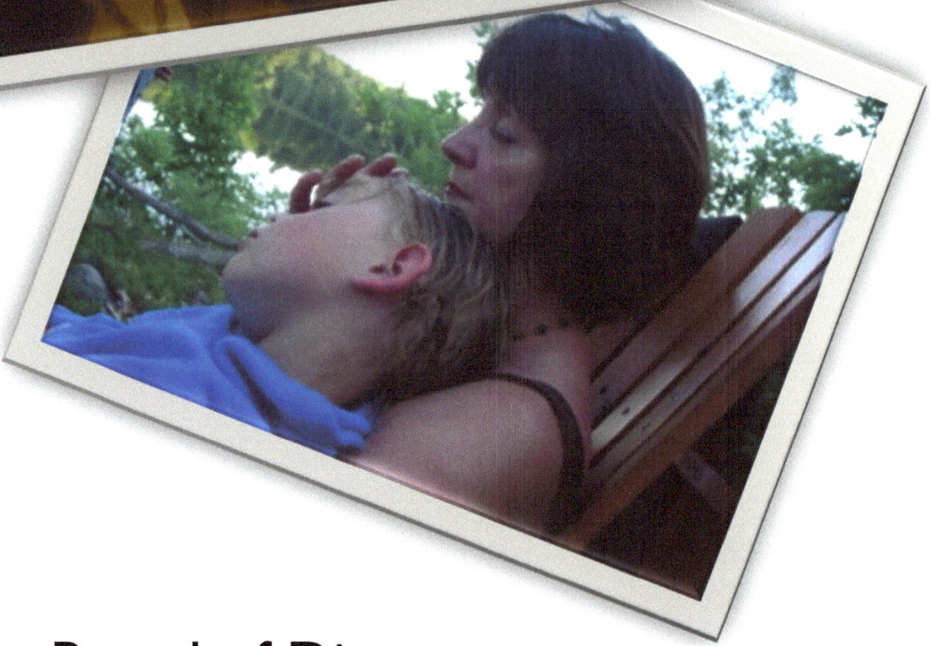

Board of Directors Handbook

2016–2018

Ideas without action are useless.

– *Harvey Mackay*

I long to accomplish a great and noble task, but it is my chief duty to accomplish small tasks as if they were great and noble.

– *Helen Keller*

General Overview of the Board of Directors

The Board assumes both legal and fiduciary responsibilities for Wintergreen Studios and performs the role of trustees. It is the board that establishes the mission, values and governing policies for Wintergreen.

Recruitment of Board Members

In the first instance, it is members of the Board who consult regarding new board members when a vacancy occurs. In addition, prospective board members are invited to apply through the Wintergreen website (info@wintergreenstudios.com).

Potential board members should:

- Be committed to the development of a sustainable society and have an affinity for the arts in all forms—the fine arts, the performing arts, the outdoor arts, and the domestic arts.
- Subscribe to the Mission Statement of Wintergreen Studios.
- Commit to a minimum of three years on the Board, and prepare for and attend all of its meetings (estimated at 3 hours every four months).
- Spend about 2 hours each month in additional Committee or Working Group.
- Meet specific skill and experience gaps as identified by the Board.
- Not represent any other organization or interest that could create a conflict of interest.
- Participate in an introductory period that includes: an exploratory interview with the Chair or designated Board member, an orientation tour of Wintergreen Studios and grounds, and participation in at least one Wintergreen program (if not involved in one previously).

Meeting Schedule

Regular meetings of the Board of Directors are held quarterly. These meetings generally occur in March, June, September and December of each year. In addition, there is an Annual General Meeting of the Board of Directors every September, when the Slate of Directors is approved.

Board members generally serve three to five year renewable terms.

Travel

Board members who travel some distance to Board meetings, which are generally held at Wintergreen or in Kingston, are compensated for mileage at the rate of $.42/km.

Records

The Secretary-Treasurer and President keep electronic records of all agendas and minutes of the Board of Directors, including those of the Finance Committee. The Secretary-Treasurer also keeps electronic copies of receipts issued for charitable donations.

Past financial records are kept at Wintergreen and at Queen's University with the Executive Director. Current financial records are kept at Queen's University and with Wintergreen's bookkeeper.

Other Wintergreen documents, such as articles of incorporation, permits, inspections, etc., are kept at Queen's University. There, a sample of marketing materials are also housed. Archived records, such as those detailing construction permits, plans, and costs, are kept at Queen's University.

Electronic databases are kept through Campaign Monitor and Wufoo. These are downloaded and printed periodically for reviewing and archival purposes.

Board of Directors

Founding Directors and Current Directors

The directors have accumulated many decades of experience as artists, writers, musicians, craftspeople, researchers, educators, and administrators. They have worked in university settings, for public institutions, in the broadcast industry, for private educational institutions, and in public schools throughout Canada, the United States, Europe, Africa, and Australia.

Rena Upitis (Founding President)

Dr. Rena Upitis (Ed.D., Harvard) is Professor of Education at Queen's University and recently completed a six-year term as National Research Co-director of Learning Through the Arts, a multi-year project that brings artists to the classrooms of over 160,000 students. She is a former Dean of Education at Queen's University (1995-2000). Rena's research and curriculum projects have explored teacher, artist, and student transformation through the arts. Rena is a timber-frame carpenter, and has a small design practice specializing in ecologically sensitive designs and materials for residents and retreats. Her current research explores ways that students can develop ecological habits of mind through arts explorations and web-based portfolio tools. She is also Principal Investigator for the iSCORE project, a research and development program for online digital music tools.

Serena Manson (Founding Vice-President; current Director)

Serena Manson (B.Ed., Queen's University) is a former teacher with Mulberry School, a developing Waldorf school in Kingston, and currently a graduate student at Queen's University. She strives to develop and research curricula that are of service to children and to humanity, integrating the arts, environmental education and appreciation, and a kinesthetic approach to learning. Serena is an avid gardener and conservationist. For many years, she lived within the Frontenac Arch Biosphere Reserve, where Wintergreen is also located, in a heritage home that provided her with opportunities to engage in renovation, building, and design. She and her partner and child now reside in Kingston, Ontario.

Helen Turnbull (Founding Secretary; currently Secretary-Treasurer)

Helen Turnbull (B.Ed., Queen's) retired as a Principal with Kawartha Pine Ridge District School Board. She brings over a decade of administrative experience to the position. Helen has been involved with curriculum development for nearly three decades, including the co-creation, with Rena Upitis, of a high-school cooperative placement program at the Wintergreen site for students in French Immersion. This award-winning program ran for three years in the mid-1990s at Wintergreen before being located at the Ganaraska Forest Centre. Helen lives in a heritage home near Gores Landing, Ontario, and has also been involved in extensive building, renovation, and design projects.

Ann Patteson (Founding Treasurer; term ended September 2010)

Dr. Ann Patteson (Ph.D., Queen's) recently retired as the International/National Director of Research for Learning Through the Arts (LTTA) at The Royal Conservatory of Music (Toronto). Ann brings twenty-five years of experience as an educator of adults to her work at Wintergreen. In her research, Ann explores the impact of arts-infused education, as well as how the arts may foster understanding of human responsibility to all of earth's inhabitants and the environment.

Katharine Smithrim (Founding Director; currently Vice-President)

Dr. Katharine Smithrim (Ph.D., Eastman) taught courses in music and the arts at Queen's University. She is now Professor Emerita of Queen's University. Over the last thirty years she has taught music programs privately, and in schools, community colleges and universities. In the 1980s Katharine pioneered music programs for parents with babies and toddlers in Toronto. Along with Bob McGrath of Sesame Street, she has made two commercial recordings: The Baby Record and Songs and Games for Toddlers, the latter a Juno nominee and now a Golden Book Video. Her recent research has focuses on spiritual dimensions in teaching and learning.

Lawrence Scanlan (Current Director)

A writer and editor and a veteran journalist, Lawrence Scanlan's most recent book, *A Year of Living Generously,* is about philanthropy and generosity of spirit. It was published by Douglas &McIntyre in the spring of 2010. The eldest of eight siblings, Lawrence Scanlan grew up in a three-bedroom, bunk bed-filled bungalow in a Toronto suburb. His father ran the church hockey and baseball leagues and his sons would all become coaches and his daughters all volunteered in the community. His mother, a geriatric nurse, set an example of understated compassion. When she died several years ago, Lawrence began to ponder her legacy, the mark we humans make in this world and the role of generosity in our daily lives. His most recent book is the outcome of that pondering. Lawrence has been a journalist for almost four decades, working with daily newspapers (editor of *The Nelson Daily News* in B.C., literary editor of *The Whig-Standard* in Ontario), magazines (managing editor of *Harrowsmith),* and in radio with two national CBC programs (producer on Morningside and Writers & Company). He has won numerous prizes for his writing, including three National Magazine Awards. Lawrence is the author or co-author of fifteen books, on subjects ranging from horses to hockey to home. He has a home in Kingston, Ontario, and a cabin in Prince Edward County.

Honorary Patrons

Lorna Crozier

Lorna Crozier has published 14 books of poetry which have garnered Canada's top awards, including the Governor-General's Award, two Pat Lowther Awards and the National Magazine Award's Gold Medal for Poetry. She is a Distinguished Professor at the University of Victoria and a fellow of the Royal Society of Canada. In 2005 she read at a command performance for Queen Elizabeth II. Her most recent work, *The Book of Marvels*, defies categorization — it is poetry, essay, fact, and fiction. Her publisher describes it as "a series of playful and startling prose meditations, celebrated writer Lorna Crozier brings her rapt attention to the small matter of household objects: everything from doorknobs, washing machinesand zippers to the kitchen sink." Two universities have awarded Lorna honorary doctorates for her contribution to Canadian literature, and in 2011 she was invested as an Officer of the Order of Canada. She is a frequent guest on CBC radio and has read her poetry on every continent except Antarctica. A bilingual Spanish edition of her poems called *La Perspectiva Del Gato* was published in Mexico in 2009. Her most recent publication is *Small Beneath the Sky, A Prairie Memoir*. Her poems have been set to music, made into a film and used as themes in paintings and pottery. She conducted writing retreats at Wintergreen in the summers of 2010 and 2011 to much acclaim. Called "a poet to be grateful for" by Margaret Laurence, she has been an ambassador for poetry wherever she goes.

Lawrence Hill

Lawrence Hill is the son of American immigrants—a black father and a white mother—who came to Canada the day after they married in 1953 in Washington, D.C. On his father's side, Hill's grandfather and great grandfather were university-educated, ordained ministers of the African Methodist Episcopal Church. His mother came from a Republican family in Oak Park, Illinois, graduated from Oberlin College and went on to become a civil rights activist. The story of how they met, married, left the United States and raised a family in Toronto is described in Hill's bestselling memoir *Black Berry, Sweet Juice: On Being Black and White in Canada*. Much of Hill's writing touches on issues of identity and belonging. Lawrence Hill's third novel was published as *The Book of Negroes* in Canada and the UK, and as *Someone Knows My Name* in the USA, Australia and New Zealand. It won the overall Commonwealth Writers' Prize for Best Book, the Rogers Writers' Trust Fiction Prize, and the Ontario Library Association's Evergreen Award. Hill is also the author of the novels *Any Known Blood* and *Some Great Thing*. A recent non-fiction book, *The Deserter's Tale: the Story of an Ordinary Soldier Who Walked Away from the War in Iraq* (written with Joshua Key), was published around the world. He is currently adapting *The Book of Negroes* for a six-part TV miniseries, and writing and preparing to deliver the 2013 Massey Lectures. Formerly a reporter with The Globe and Mail and The Winnipeg Free Press, Hill has lived and worked across Canada, in Baltimore, and in Spain and France. He is also an honorary patron of Crossroads International, for which he travelled as a volunteer to several West African countries. Hill is also a member of the Council of Patrons of the Black Loyalist Heritage Society, and of the Advisory Council of Book Clubs for Inmates. He has a B.A. in economics from Laval University and an M.A. in writing from Johns Hopkins University. Hill lives in Hamilton, Ontario.

Organization Chart

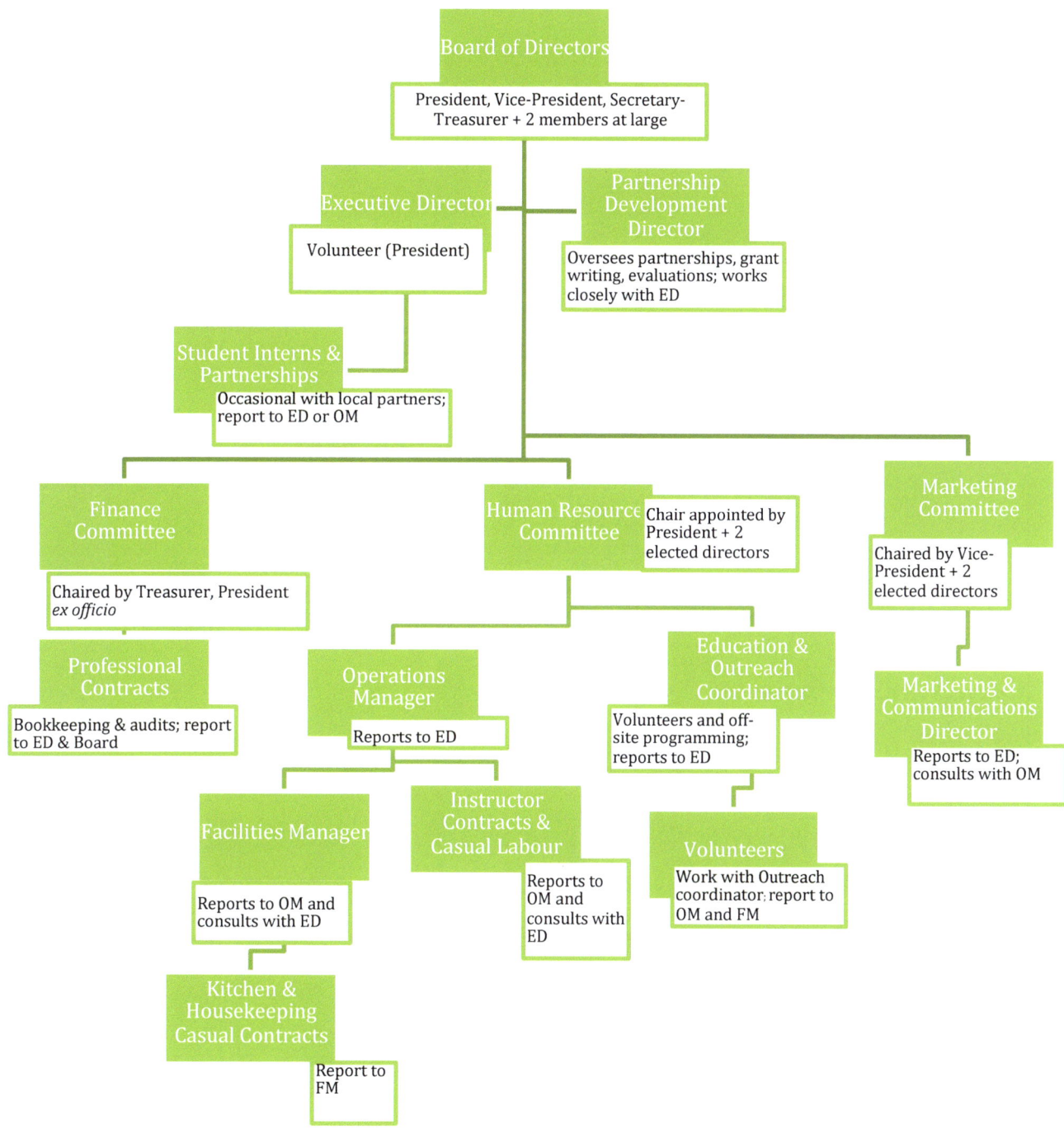

Board Committees

Finance Committee

Chair: Secretary-Treasurer

Members: President, Partnership Development Officer

Meeting Schedule: Generally in August before the September Board Meeting and AGM

The Finance Committee is responsible for:

- ✓ Developing the Annual Budget
- ✓ Vetting and approving the Year-end Financial Statements
- ✓ Providing recommendations to the Board for any acquisitions or expenditures outside the approved budget
- ✓ Setting policies for travel
- ✓ Setting policies for signing authority

Human Resource Committee

Chair: Vice-President

Members: President, Member-at-Large

Meeting Schedule: Fall of each year for programs decisions; as needed for employment

---

The Human Resource Committee is responsible for:

- ✓ Vetting and approving staff job descriptions
- ✓ Recruiting and selecting staff for positions that become available
- ✓ Developing criteria for hiring instructors
- ✓ Conducting annual reviews of staff members
- ✓ Developing the annual program of workshops and events

Marketing Committee

Chair: Vice-President

Members: President, Marketing & Communications Director

Meeting Schedule: As required

The Marketing Committee is responsible for:

- ✓ Developing the Annual Marketing and Communications Plan
- ✓ Administering the Annual Giving Campaign
- ✓ Maintaining and updating forms and databases
- ✓ Website development and maintenance
- ✓ Social marketing
- ✓ Overseeing print materials and advertising
- ✓ Planning and executing fund-raising campaigns and events

Wintergreen Studios Press is an independent literary press. It is affiliated with the not-for-profit educational retreat centre, Wintergreen Studios. The Press supports the work of Wintergreen Studios by publishing works related to education, culture, and the environment.

www.wintergreenstudios.com